Expanded edition with cruising t, ...included

San Juan Islands Cruise Guide

Boater's Handbook for Cruising the Islands

Copyright 2014   Compiled and written by JR Cummins

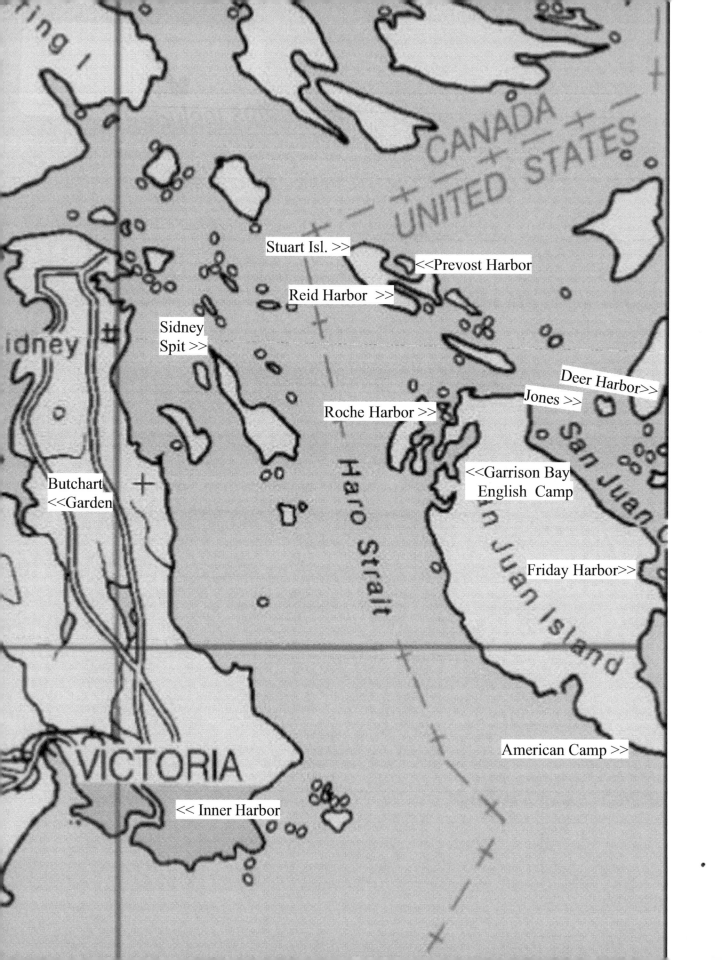

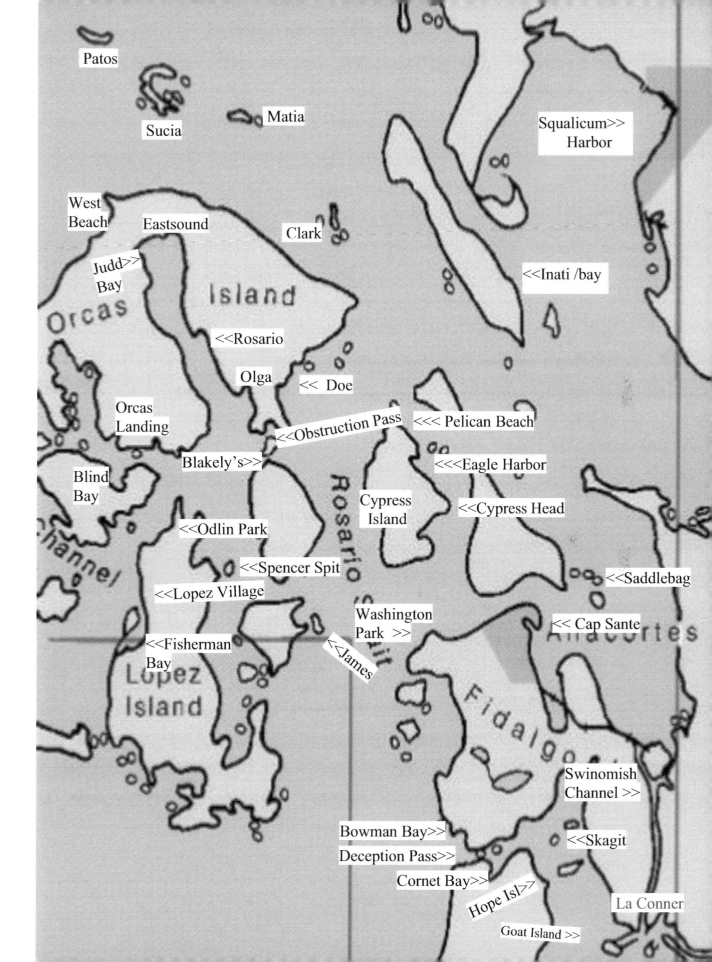

Cruising Notes

About the Author

JR Cummins lives in Portland Or, and has been an avid boater since building his first kayak for a seventh grade school project. Many boats have come and gone since, but it has been a decades long obsession with dragging his wife and children to the San Juan's that has resulted in this guidebook.

From one Boater to Another.

We first came to the San Juan's armed with a few guidebooks, and a chart. Five sailboats and two powerboats later, the same, now tattered chart is folded in its second acrylic cover, we are still making the rounds, and enjoying every minute. Over the years we have zeroed in on boat camping, gunk holing, and exploring whatever we can reach by water.

Our intention with this guidebook is to share our knowledge with other boaters, but due to the expense of a large book we, have left out reams of information and concentrated on just *"where"* to go and *"what"* to see. You will need to supply the *"who, what and why."* The pictures displayed were never intended to be published, they are of family outings, and were chosen to convey the proverbial *"thousand"* words.

The readable, *large garish labels* plastered across the map at the front of this guide are to help you stay oriented and locate all the parks and places to visit.

I invite you to visit my website www.sailingthesanjuans.com (an ongoing work) You will recognize some story's, some pictures and a general attitude. John

Preface

Places to go! Things to do! What to expect! Answers you want!

This cruising guide contains the information you need for successful cruising in the San Juan's and surrounding area. Straight forward honest descriptions and reviews of parks, marinas, and resorts where boats are the standard mode of travel and cruisers are the norm.

Deception Pass to Sucia, Friday Harbor to Butchart Garden, and all the rest in between.

Also included are sections on dealing with currents, navigating, bicycling, hiking, and all the marine campgrounds…*Plus launching ramps, where to buy fuel, mileage chart, and more.*

Warning from the author: Before writing this guide I was where some of you are now. So I read some books and cast off anyway, which is what I suggest you do asap. This guide will help you avoid some of the less fun times and zero in on great cruises. *Take heed* when reading reviews and comments, if I say a place is not worth the effort, *I may be generous*. More importantly, if I say a place is *well worth a visit*, then it is somewhere I really like and chances are *you will too*. Inside is practical and useful knowledge for cruising, not flowery sugar coated prose.

A special thanks to Linda, my wife, best friend and partner who is instrumental in every great cruise, and to Mariah, Wind Song, Quartet, Zippy, Sunshine, Rosey and Kraken, our boats to the San Juan's, so far.

CONTENTS

CONTENTS

Interpreting Cruise Ratings!

The cruise rating assigned to each location is based upon an overall visit not just specific points. For instance, if a destination has fantastic scenery and hikes, I would tend to rate it higher even though anchoring may be a bit of a pain. Conversely, easy anchoring may be a big plus but doesn't mean I like to visit the place more.

Having a dock means one you can overnight at unless noted. Not having anchor buoys doesn't mean you can't anchor, it means use your own anchor.

Hiking means hiking in the woods, not walking around town, although walking around Victoria is certainly a hike.

Having fire rings means using a vacant campsite, although I note beachfront fire rings.

Dinghy beaches are suitable for landing at all tide levels and must be close to where your headed. When boat camping a good dinghy beach is more important than bringing iced beer.

• Dock	No
• Campsites	Yes
• Water	No
• Anch. Buoys	Yes
• Hiking	Yes
• Bathroom	Yes
• Fee	Yes
• Fire rings	No
• Dinghy Beach	Yes

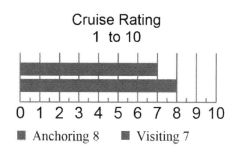

Cruise Rating
1 to 10

0 1 2 3 4 5 6 7 8 9 10

■ Anchoring 8   ■ Visiting 7

Islands, Parks, Resorts, Marinas

For easy trip planning, this guidebook is organized into four areas. North, South, East and West, just like points on a compass. The San Juan's and surrounding areas comprise all of San Juan County, plus bits and pieces of Whatcum, Skagit, and Island County's. Locations and areas are determined by commonly traveled water routes, not land areas.

West *area includes:*

South *inner island area:*

North *area includes:*

East *area:*

Eastsound is South?

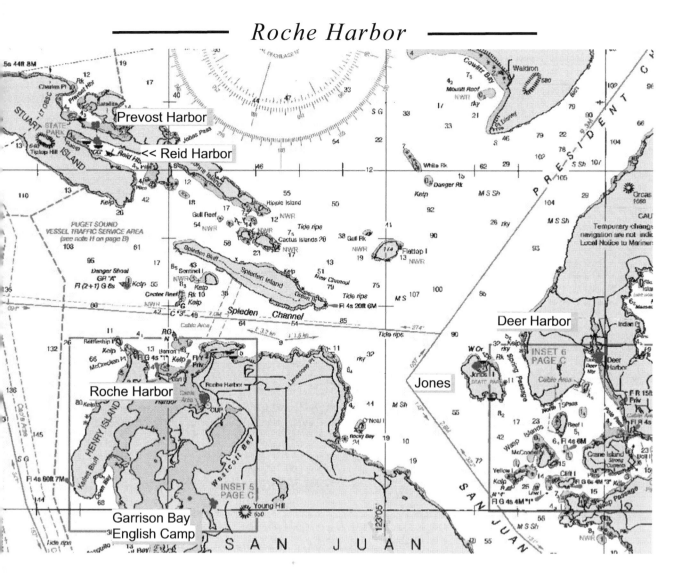

Roche harbor is not a city, it is a private resort, but is so popular that it may as well be a city. They offer customs check in, a well stocked store, restaurants, expansive floats and slips where hundred foot yachts frequent. On shore are hiking, sights, historic gardens....

Anchoring room in the bay goes on for miles. The following picture of Roche was on the 4th of July. Yes it was hectic and confusing and drove the admiral crazy, but in reality there was lots of room and you should have been there too.

Roche Harbor is considered by some to be the premier destination in the San Juans. If you're coming to the San Juans, you should make sure to visit three destinations.

Rosario, Friday Harbor, and Roche Harbor.

Tip These are the three places that you will wish you had checked out.

All body's of water, including Roche Harbor are public. During busy holidays such as the fourth of July the bay becomes one giant anchorage. Don't be surprised to see commercial passenger seaplanes landing and taxiing among the boats.

When arriving at Roche simply call the harbor master on 66 and ask for a temporary slip assignment if you just want to come ashore for a few hours, restock and walk up to the Sculpture Garden. Same thing if you plan to spend the night.

If you prefer to anchor, simply drop your hook somewhere nearby and run your dinghy over to one of two dinghy docks, then make yourself at home.

Garrison Bay & English Camp

Garrison Bay is a medium size shallow bay off Roche Harbor. Garrison is a good place to get away from the hustle of Roche for some peace and quiet, it's much smaller and so will have less of everything, especially wakes from inconsiderate dinghy drivers heading for the floats at Roche. On shore is historic "English Camp." You should check out the formal garden the troops kept tidy while stationed there. The small float makes it very easy to go ashore. Garrison Bay would be a good place to leave your boat anchored for extended periods. It would also make an excellent home base for bicycling San Juan Island.

American Camp & English Camp

You probably already know about English Camp, American Camp and the famous 13 year Pig War so we won't go into all that happened historically. Looking at maps you would think that the two camps are easily reached by boat since they both have water frontage. Let's start with American Camp, it fronts on Haro Strait but there are no amenities or anything to help a mariner half a mile out at sea trying to spot where to anchor and bring the dinghy to shore. So that being said, you can try to visit that way (by boat) but it's not worth the effort, the windswept nearly treeless site although developed with an interpretation center and somewhat popular to land based visitors is not outstanding so why bother. I will suggest that if you're bicycling from Roche or Friday, American Camp is a good bike ride destination, and then on to Cattle Point Lighthouse. Our family has biked from Friday and found the ride easy and worthwhile because we were going for a bike ride, not a history lesson. In all fairness, American Camp also fronts on Griffin Bay and there is reputed to be a trail, but we spent half a day and two shore landings trying to find our way across a swamp and through the woods, before finally giving up. Five years later we arrived by bicycle on a paved road, mission accomplished.

English Camp

This is where the English made their very proper military camp and headquarters along the shore of appropriately named Garrison Bay. The restored heritage site is a gentle breeze of a walk from the small float. We recommend you stop by for a quick visit. Refined cruisers will find Garrison Bay a welcome and peaceful overnight anchorage just around the corner from unruly Roche Harbor. English Camp is complete with manicured gardens and military stockade type buildings. From the top of Officers Hill you can see the parade grounds and get a picture of your boat. Take the dinghy to shore or bring the mother ship into the small dock if there is room. See for yourself where the British soldiers lived that almost went to war because a pig ate some potatoes growing in a garden that belonged to the other side. Oh, did I mention the pig was the only casualty? He got shot! It's unclear if he was eaten.

Deer Harbor ───

W ay, way on the far side, and yet still on the inside, but even beyond West Sound is Deer Harbor. You will find a marina and fuel dock plus a small deli grocery on the wharf. That pretty much sums up what most boaters will want. They have overnight slips but on some summer weekends will likely need to be reserved in advance. There is a county dock adjacent to the fuel dock for your use. (that means, after you take on fuel, just shove your boat forward a few boat lengths and you are at the county dock and can now tie up and walk around.) Up the ramp at the end of the wharf are restrooms and a laundry. The large bay has, room to anchor anytime, and anywhere. Deer Harbor is very close to Jones Island, so it is the obvious choice when making a run for ice or an expensive bottle of cheap wine. Just kidding, they have expensive bottles of expensive wine also.

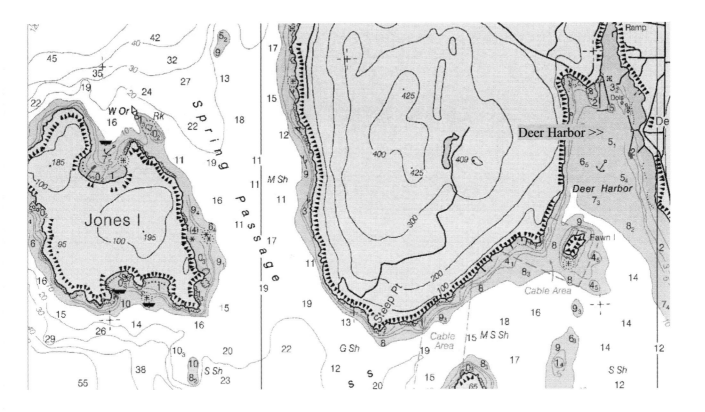

Deer Harbor's close proximity to Jones Island makes it very easy to run for groceries in the dinghy or kayak, it also explains the popularity of Jones for kayakers paddling from Deer Harbor.

If you come to the San Juans with kayaks on the roof of your car to go camping, Deer Harbor is an excellent choice for starting your paddle, and Jones is an excellent destination. There are excursion guides operating out of Deer Harbor and kayaks for rent.

Jones Island State Park

Rating
1 to 10

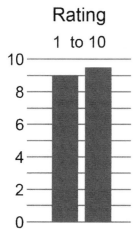

● Dock	Yes
● Campsites	Yes
● Water	Yes
● Anch. Buoys	Yes
● Hiking	Yes
● Bathroom	Yes
● Fee	Yes
● Fire rings	Yes
● Dinghy Beach	Yes

■ Anchoring 9

■ Visiting 9.5

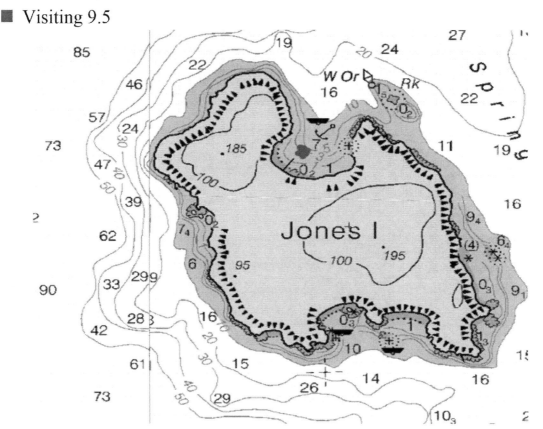

Jones Island is the #1 place to take your family and enjoy boat camping. The islands unique proximity to the three major Marinas and harbors in the San Juans is a big plus, but even without these great nearby neighbors, Jones would still be your destination of choice.

All Jones is a state park, the north cove is preferred by power boaters and sailors alike sharing a protected bay, dock and anchor buoys. If the buoys are in use it is easy to anchor more boats. The south cove is favored by kayaker's where there are group sites and Adirondack shelters. The island has running water, fire pits and picnic tables. On a sunny summer weekend it would not be unusual to find several large kayaker groups camping. The south cove is not protected from San Juan Channel traffic or swells, so anchoring or using the buoys there will be a crap shoot. Jones has several well mannered hiking trails, rated, easy and moderate. From the trails are outstanding views of the surrounding islands, and waters. Bring your camera to Jones, you will want to preserve the memories to show your friends that aren't as fortunate as you.

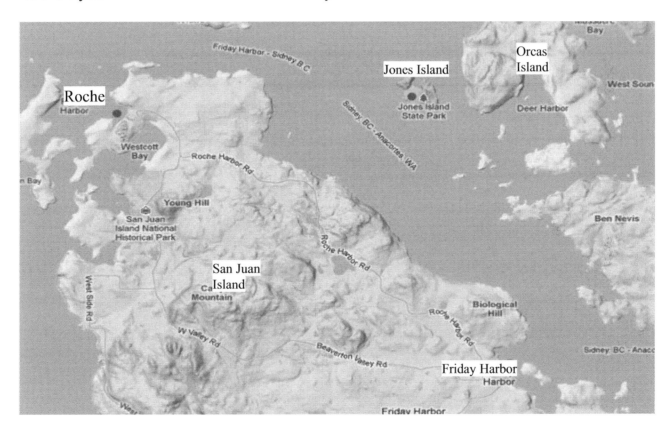

As a place to anchor, Jones rates a 9
As a place to visit a 9.5
Crowds sometimes make a visit difficult
but we have never left unable to anchor.

9+9.5 wow

The friendly little deer are legendary on Jones. I say little because they are noticeably smaller than the deer on other islands. Some (not all) are tame as house pets begging for handouts, allowing petting and ear rubs.

The south side has a number of more primitive campsites for human and wind powered vessels, plus large group sites and shelters. The wind coming off the water can be nasty here, while the other side of the island is serene and peaceful.

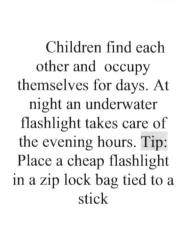

Children find each other and occupy themselves for days. At night an underwater flashlight takes care of the evening hours. Tip: Place a cheap flashlight in a zip lock bag tied to a stick

The north cove has a newer dock, and a spot just for dinghies, but the gravel beach is excellent too. Anchor buoys are in the bay but there is plenty of room to anchor and save the fee. The cove is protected from all but the worst north winds. On shore are lots of tent sites, many are shore front, each with picnic table and fire rings. There is a nice mowed lawn area for games and grazing deer. Bathrooms are clean and convenient, drinking water is cool and tastes good. There is not much negative about Jones Island.

It's easy to wile away the days

13

— Stuart Island State Park —

Reid Harbor
Prevost Harbor

• Dock	Yes
• Campsites	Yes
• Water	No
• Anch. Buoys	Yes
• Hiking	Yes
• Bathroom	Yes
• Fee	Yes
• Fire rings	Yes
• Dinghy Beach	No

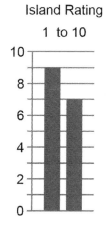

Island Rating
1 to 10

■ Anchoring 9
■ Visiting 7

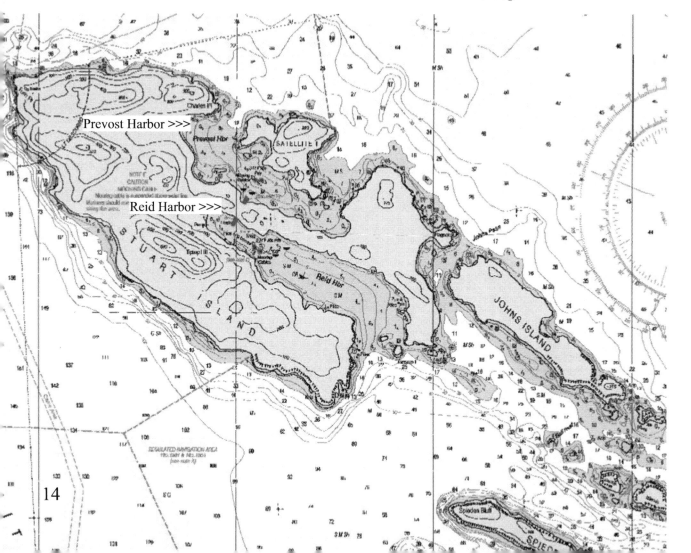

Prevost Harbor >>>

Reid Harbor >>>

Turn Point Lighthouse

Stuart Island State Park

<< Two docks are at Reid and Prevost Harbors

W ay, way over on the other side of Orcas and just a little north of Roche Harbor is where you will find Stuart Island, with *Turn Point* jutting out into Haro Strait marking the NW corner of Washington State. The island is mostly private property but the state maintains a park on a narrow isthmus between Prevost and Reid Harbors. We decide which bay (Reid or Prevost) to go to pretty much based on whim, or where we may be headed later. Roche Harbor is just a straight shot and very fast to and from, and if you hitch a ride with a favorable current, you can almost drift back and forth. We have observed youthful cruisers rowing skiffs full of camping gear from Roche. A skiff is what a becalmed 15' daysailer becomes when the wind dies. Getting to Prevost on the other side is more distance, time and work, but if your already spending the day sailing in Haro or Boundary Pass then so much the better. Out in the harbors are anchoring buoys and floats. The two anchorages although separate are joined at the hip. Both harbors have their own dock and gangplank leading to a shared campground, bathrooms and trail system.

The hike up to the schoolhouse and beyond to Turn Point Lighthouse is the main shore side activity besides having campfires in vacant camp sites. (See the section on hiking and strolling)

Float at Reid Harbor

When hiking to the Lighthouse you will walk by this newer one room school house on Stuart Island. The older much smaller one next to it is now a little museum.

16

Orcas Landing and Blind Bay ———

Orcas Island

Y ou need to be aware of Orcas Landing if you don't have a holding tank. Most likely you will drive by and miss it completely because it is right next to the ferry terminal. I avoid ferries and so should you, but the short term, 30 minute dock is a handy crossroads pit stop. At the top of the plank is ice and groceries and across the street is a public restroom. Expect auto and pedestrian traffic lining up to catch the ferry. The float is unprotected and your boat will be battered by waves and wakes while tied up, but you can tie on the inside which will help a little.

Visit Orcas Landing and then anchor across the way at Blind Bay, between both places you can have a decent destination with a bathroom.

Tip miss the rocks at the entrance to Blind Bay

Not much at Blind Bay but a mostly protected place to anchor. I think a lot of people are reluctant to anchor just any old place like me so big open bays seem to attract lots of customers. Of course across the channel is Orcas Landing where you are not supposed to overnight at the dock so Blind Bay is the perfect spot for them. The image below is both Blind Bay and Orcas Landing. Paddling a dinghy over to Orcas from Blind Bay is ill advised but possible. The current through Harney Channel could whisk you away, but that's how exploring and discovering works. However in four to six hours the current may bring you and the dinghy back.

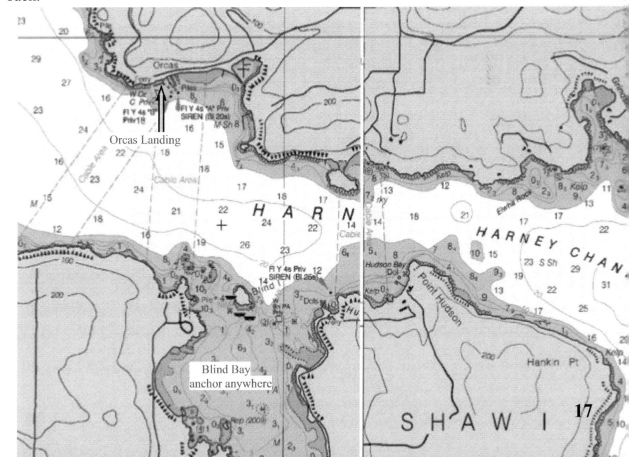

F riday Harbor is the one place you should go if you can only go to one place. Go to Friday Harbor if you come by ferry, sailboat, or airplane. Go on foot or bicycle. Go. Go. Go.

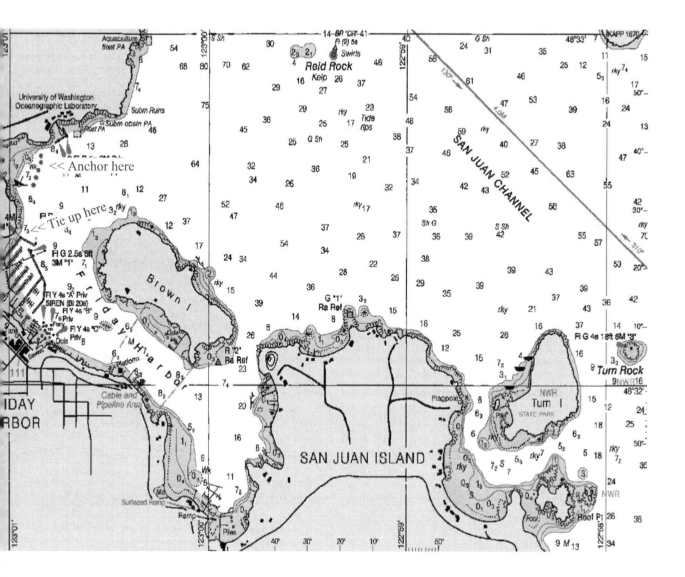

When arriving by boat, you will be presented with a bustling seaport, ferries will be moving in and out and seaplanes may land or take to the air beside you. The dock you want is to the far right, ferry and airplanes are to the left. At the far outside (on the right) is a breakwater float for short term and overflow tie ups. You may grab a spot anywhere on either side, boats are pulling out constantly, if you wait a minute you will get a spot. If you want you may call the harbormaster

on channel 66 and request a short term or overnight slip, short term slip assignments are complimentary, but overnight will cost about $1.50 per foot..

We routinely park short term and walk into town for a restaurant fix or to buy trinkets and provisions. Of course having nice clean public restrooms out on the float is a big plus.
Tip: Consider staying every night of your cruise at Friday, making day trips to the outer parks and islands. You could even walk to a motel or bed and breakfast and never sleep or eat on the boat. (Cruisers with fifty footers don't rough it, why should you!) FYI the dinghy dock is near the gangplank (aren't they all?) Every Saturday morning, April through September is a Farmers Market at the Brickworks Plaza. Bring your appetite for breakfast or lunch and feast on the island cuisine, then bring home locally made arts and crafts. Tip: Don't miss Friday Harbor.

Friday Harbor

Lopez Village

Lopez Village >>

• Dock	No
• Campsites	No
• Water	No
• Anch. Buoys	No
• Strolling	Yes
• Bathroom	Yes
• Fee	No
• Fire rings	No
• Dinghy Beach	Yes

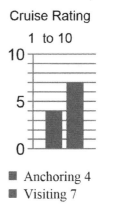

Cruise Rating

1 to 10

■ Anchoring 4
■ Visiting 7

Lopez Village

In the San Juan's there are only a few places to visit where you can join in with the motor vehicle crowd and mingle amongst land borne tourists. Whether it be dining in bistros or shopping in trendy shops, Friday Harbor, La Conner, East Sound and Lopez Village pretty much are your only choices. Lopez Village is mostly overlooked because walking from the Islander Resort in Fisherman Bay is a tad bit too far to walk and then bring back a full stomach or arm load of souvenirs, let alone bags of provisions for the boat.

It doesn't have to be a long arduous walk, you can go by dinghy and land downtown only a hundred feet from the fudge shop, or about a block to the main grocery store. As a big bonus across the street from where you come ashore is the public restrooms complete with free showers (donations accepted).

Directions to Lopez Village:

Look on the map above for the red dot. That's where Lopez Village is located. The gravel beach is dinghy friendly and you will use the galvanized steel stairway as a landmark as well as your stairway up the bank. The stairs are public and a good place to tie the dinghy. On your chart you can locate the stairs by looking almost straight towards shore from the dolphin with the navigation aid marking the entrance to Fisherman Bay. You can anchor anywhere you want but you should expect good-sized wakes from vessels coming in or out of Fisherman Bay. Or simply pull inside the bay (watch the depth) where there will be no wakes, (smaller wakes) anchor anywhere and come back the short distance in the dinghy. Going by dinghy beats the heck out of trudging down the highway and makes purchasing trinkets or provisions practical.

The beach is public from the stairs south towards the bay for only one block. At the south end is an unmarked access to a public mostly sand parking lot (lowbank) This would be a good place to bring bicycles ashore if you don't want to carry them up the stairs, or run them down to the resort, your choice.

Lopez Village is just barely big enough to give you a bevy of choices from sweets to clothing or sit down food all the way to a large well stocked community grocery store, and yet it's small enough that you can cover everything on foot in under thirty minutes. That's under thirty minutes if you skip the museum, don't shower and not enter any shops. I prefer to sit at the top of the stairs and read while the crew explores.

This is what you look for from the boat, notice the stairs are galvanized and the pile of rocks in front!

Tip: In Lopez Village look for the "Lopez Farmers Market" next door to the community center. Open 10am to 2pm mid May into September every Saturday. Have lunch and pick up some local produce and seafood. Crafts people and artists will be displaying their work.

Spencer Spit State Park

Lopez Island

Cruise Rating

1 to 10

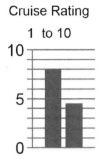

■ Anchoring 8
■ Visiting 4.5

● Dock	No
● Campsites	Yes
● Water	No
● Anch. Buoys	Yes
● Hiking	Yes
● Bathroom	Yes
● Fee	Yes
● Fire rings	No
● Dinghy Beach	Yes

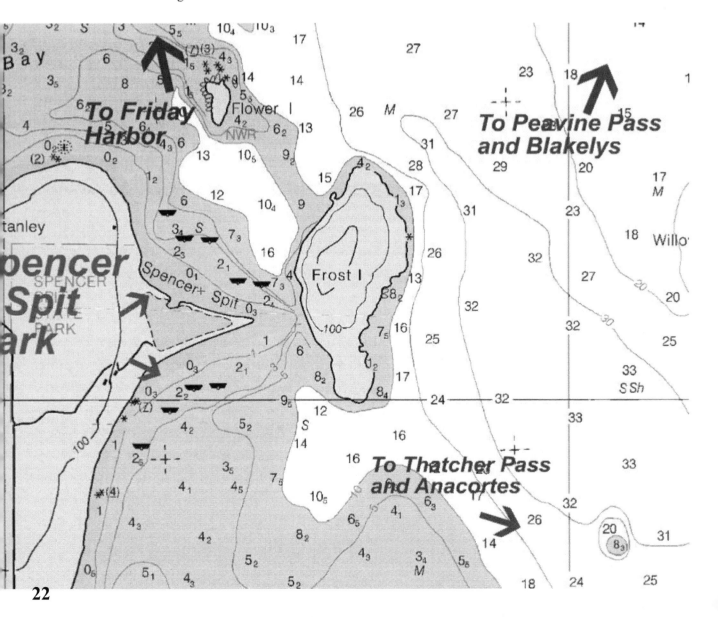

Located on the east side of Lopez Island just inside Thatcher Pass, you will likely drive past Spencer Spit many times on your way to and from Anacortes and Friday Harbor. There is no dock but lots of anchor buoys and room for many boats. On shore are campsites and bathrooms. The park is popular with car campers, and the ferry landing is close by. Bicycle rentals for exploring Lopez Island are available also. The narrow channel between the end of the spit and Frost Island is deep and easily navigated; rumor has it that a ferry captain once took his ferry through the passage but I'll let you take a look and decide if there's any truth there. Both sides of the spit are subject to wakes from passing boats although Frost island offers some protection. If the wind is up you will feel it here. Shore bathrooms are a dinghy ride and very long walk.

I've never seen the big attraction drawing people to Spencer Spit, but it
seems to have a lot of supporters, judging by the number of boats anchored.

Spencer Spit

Spencer Spit State Park, is both a marine and land accessed park. Unfortunately the state has put their resources into the land side of the equation leaving boaters with nothing but a large anchoring field and a number of anchor buoys. I don't have lots of positive things to say except anchoring is easy with acres of room. The spit is best described like all spits are described, barren and windswept, except Spencer's has a marsh in one area you are supposed to stay out of forcing a roundabout walk to the real shore up to a quarter mile away. The wind does not blow much in the summer in the inner island area *except at Spencer Spit,* where I think a campfire would be difficult, but because it's a spit you can always avoid a lee shore. I wouldn't make a big effort to visit, maybe just stop by for a quick lunch.

"This replica of the Spencer cabin is out on the very end of the spit. That's it!"

On shore is a concession that rents bicycles. (maybe that's the attraction.) Lopez Island is the most bicycle friendly of the three that people bike (San Juan and Orcas are the others) The close proximity to Thatcher Pass and Rosario Strait make Spencer Spit a good place to wait for daylight or the fog to lift before continuing. Since I brought up bicycling, I need to comment that I would not bring my bike to Spencer to begin an island bike ride, it's just too much trouble getting a two wheeler to shore and then lugging it a half mile, instead I would go to Odlin Park or one of the marinas inside Fisherman Bay so that I could use a dock to unload the bicycles.

Follow me to to Odlin Park, we can bicycle there!

Odlin County Park float on Lopez Island is perfect for
getting bicycles on and off the boat.

Odlin County Park

Lopez Island

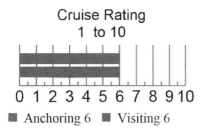

Cruise Rating
1 to 10

0 1 2 3 4 5 6 7 8 9 10

■ Anchoring 6 ■ Visiting 6

• Dock	Yes
• Campsites	Yes
• Water	Yes
• Anch. Buoys	Yes
• Hiking	Yes
• Bathroom	Yes
• Fee	Yes
• Fire rings	Yes
• Dinghy Beach	Yes
• Launch Ramp	Yes

Sandy beach and a lonely dock await you at Odlin County Park, except you can't overnight at the float, but you can anchor so close you might almost jump across, almost!

You can see Odlin has a nice beach, but that water in the background is the mainline to and from Friday Harbor so you will feel some wave action when anchored.

Odlin County Park
Lopez Island

I say lonely because we never see many boaters here, probably because we rock and roll all night, Lopez village is too far to walk but an easy 20-30 minute bike ride. What we do is offload the bikes and then anchor as close as we want, then drag the dinghy up onto the float. This way we're not hogging the dock, and our home sweet home is waiting for us when we get back dog tired. The parks four buoys are $10-$12. Just a short walk takes you to bathrooms and the campground.

Tip: Odlin County Park would be an excellent place to meet up with friends that are car camping in the San Juans. Be sure to check on reservations for camping. In a pinch your friends could camp at Spencer Spit, its just a short drive. I know your thinking why not meet at Spencer Spit State Park, you can except there's no dock there, but you have a dinghy so check on reservations at Spencer also.

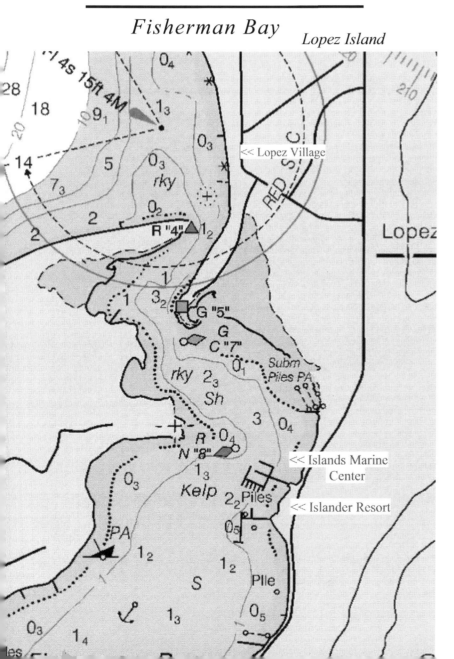

Fisherman Bay — *Lopez Island*

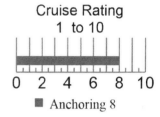

Cruise Rating
1 to 10

0 2 4 6 8 10

■ Anchoring 8

Get your boat parts and repairs at Islands Marine Center plus transient dock space.

Get your fuel, restaurant food, transient space and resort favors at Islander resort next door.

Get your shoes on, the walk into Lopez Village is .75 miles. Walk into town eat breakfast, walk back, eat lunch. Rest your feet (Or see below)

Get in the dinghy run up to the beach opposite the village and save the walk. (See the Lopez Village section for detailed directions)

Tip: watch the tide level getting in and out of the bay entrance, you may be in for a surprise and need to time your escape. Actually you should watch your bottom everywhere in the bay.

27

Rating

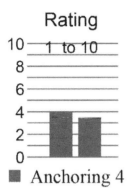

10 ┬── 1 to 10
8 ┼────────
6 ┼────────
4 ┼──■──■──
2 ┼──█──█──
0 ┴────────

■ Anchoring 4

■ Visiting 3.5

- Dock   Yes
- Campsites   No
- Water   No
- Anch. Buoys   No
- Hiking   No
- Bathroom   No
- Fee   Yes
- Fire rings   No
- Dinghy Beach Yes

What can I say! There's just nothing to holler about at Olga except maybe the lone restaurant way up a long hill. It is peaceful, but so are church's and graveyards. I don't recommend that you stop here unless you have a plan. You could plan to sit and read all day, we did. You could plan to unload a bicycle and head off, I did that too. You could pretend there was no where else to go and you are caught with the sun making it's last gasp before plunging you into absolute darkness. That works but come on. Tip: if your riding your bike to the top of Mt Constitution, Olga is the closest starting point. Now that's a plan worth hollering about.

Kraken at Olga

Eastsound and Judd Bay

- Dock — Yes
- Campsites — No
- Water — No
- Anch. Buoys — No
- Hiking — Yes
- Bathroom — No
- Fee — No
- Fire rings — No
- Dinghy Beach — No

Cruise Rating
1 to 10

0 1 2 3 4 5 6 7 8 9 10

■ Anchoring 5.5   ■ Visiting 7.5

Eastsound is not a harbor, its a city. Its the biggest and main gathering spot on Orcas Island. We have spent some enjoyable hours listening to home grown musicians and checking out craft and artist goods in local shops. I recommend you plan a visit.

There is no fuel, nor is there a suitable place to bring your dinghy ashore, except out on the point where the county built a public dock and small float. You can tie up and walk to town where you will find a large full service grocery store that everyone on the island uses. The walk is a short two blocks. Your not supposed to over night at the float, but you can anchor very close by. Those anchoring may find some waves if the wind is blowing up East Sound, there's a pretty long fetch starting all the way down in Lopez Sound to get the swells rolling.

Tip: Anchor in nearby Judd Bay but pay attention to depths in the back. Don't assume when you get to Eastsound during flat *calm* conditions that it will last through the night.

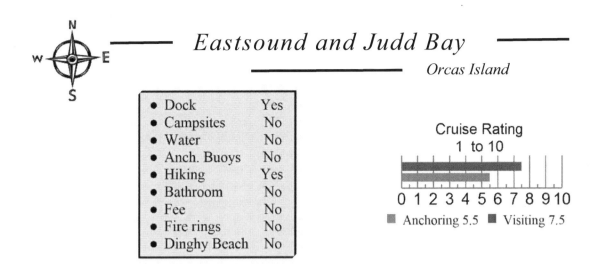

Don't miss the "Orcas Island Farmers Market" in Eastsound on the Village Green, Open every Saturday from 10am to 3pm May through October. Crafts, Arts, food.

Day use dock and >>> Access to Eastsound

Fishing Bay

Madro

Judd Bay

<< Anchor here for protection

LOCAL MAGNETIC DISTURBANCE

Rosario

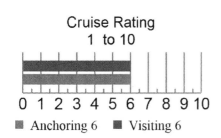

Cruise Rating
1 to 10

0 1 2 3 4 5 6 7 8 9 10

■ Anchoring 6   ■ Visiting 6

• Dock	Yes
• Campsites	No
• Water	Yes
• Anch. Buoys	Yes
• Hiking	yes
• Bathroom	Yes
• Fee	Yes
• Fire rings	no
• Dinghy Beach	no

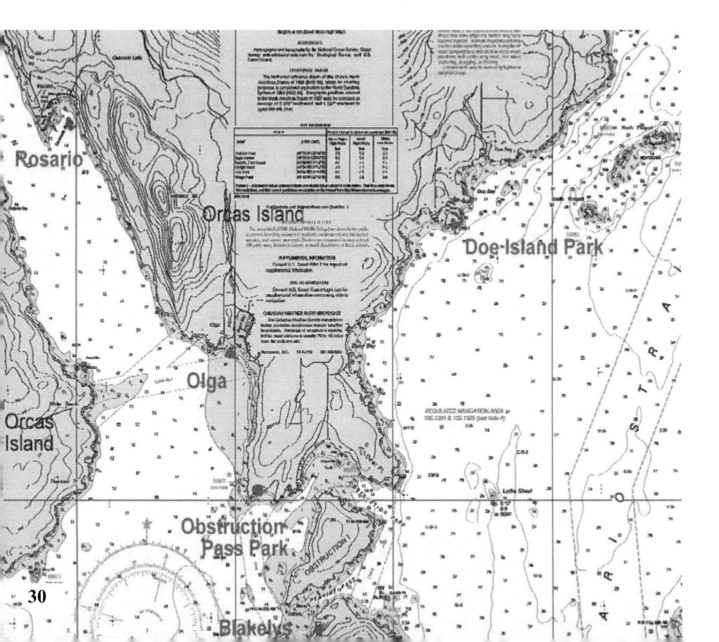

Rosario

Orcas Island

Orcas Island

Doe-Island Park

Olga

Obstruction
Pass Park

Blakelys

Rosario once was a private residence, and the original mansion is now used as a museum and restaurant. When visiting don't be surprised to see large groups attending weddings and other events. The natural bay has been turned into a small marina with rental slips, and anchor buoys off shore. The anchor buoys and the free open anchoring area are open to the sound, the marina slips are not, nuff said? (hint -- open to the sound means, open to wakes and waves) On the float is a fuel dock, nestled on the manicured lawns are tame deer, a cafe and small grocery and gift store. Stop for an hour or a day or overnight. Visiting Rosario is the one place your friends will ask you about, it seems to have developed a mystique that has traveled to non boaters.

Rosario Resort is much talked about and highly touted as the place to go of all places. My perspective is somewhat different. First of all, yes you should go there and tour the mansion and free museum if you have any interest at all in the areas history. Secondly there is nothing at all wrong with their store, fuel dock, restaurants, or marina slips, and very tame pet-able deer wander the spacious grounds. Thirdly we always enjoy stopping by, but that doesn't make it the fourth wonder of the world.

Rosario is located part way in on the right side of East Sound, just a rock skip past the community of Olga. The well stocked store has slightly elevated prices, but after all it's Rosario don't cha know. The large two sided fuel dock is easy to get in and out of regardless of wind direction. The staff is very friendly and once let us leave the boat at the main dock, (we just pushed it past the fuel area) while we bicycled three+ hours to Moran State Park. They won all the points that day. Tip: Rosario (like Roche and Friday) is one of those places you have to visit sooner or later to be a complete San Juan cruiser.

Obstruction Pass

Rating

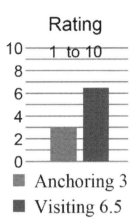

10 — 1 to 10
8
6
4
2
0

■ Anchoring 3
■ Visiting 6.5

Take a good look at your chart and imagine the fetch waves and swells have coming all the way from the south end of Lopez sound. This is a difficult place to make your boats settle down, but once you are ashore there is a nice group of coves to explore with views to Olga, Rosario and beyond. The lee shore beach gets tossed high with storm driven driftwood. Up in the woods are campsites and bathrooms. The highway brings campers, hikers and bikers so expect to find people without boats wandering the forest just like you. I would definitely come here for a day visit, but spending the night at the anchor buoys or setting my own hook would be sadistic if you still have a crew or mate. Tip: anywhere you see piles of driftwood is a warning to watch out. You may be next!

● Dock	No
● Campsites	Yes
● Water	No
● Anch. Buoys	Yes
● Hiking	Yes
● Bathroom	Yes
● Fee	Yes
● Fire rings	Yes
● Dinghy Beach	Yes

Blakely's

Blakely's Marina and Store

*N*ow here is a place you will really appreciate! A perceptive reader and savvy cruiser will notice that sentence, or should I repeat myself ? Blakely Island is private so you will not be going anywhere outside the marina grounds. The first time I purchased fuel at the dock there was no one around so I asked a local fisherman before he pulled away what the procedure was and he said, "Just put the gas in your boat and remember how much you get, then walk up to the store and tell them how much you got." That first purchase at Blakely's was fifteen gallons of gas, five huge ice cream cones and a bunch of Hershey bars. I think our most recent visit was just for ice cream.

Blakely's is located inside Peavine Pass around the corner just enough so that when Rosario Strait is throwing hissy fits, the float is calm and welcoming.

When you are heading from Anacortes or Bellingham to Friday Harbor or other places it is very convenient to swing in, when the south end of Rosario is fogged in forcing you north around Cypress Island, again you will appreciate Blakely's central location.

The fuel and store float is fairly long accommodating many boats and because it is accessible from both sides you will always be able to have a favorable approach regardless of wind and current. The transient slips are inside a small much-protected bay assuring a peaceful rest. Tip: Blakely's belongs on your short list.

Doe Island

*D*oe Island may be the smallest developed State Park in the San Juans. Its diminutive size makes it hard to spot on charts, Google Earth or when you are floating a half mile offshore and staring right at it. Sitting just a few hundred feet off the east side of Orcas and just two miles or so north of Obstruction Pass, it's a side trip you should not miss. Stop there as a lunch stop or overnight-er. On shore are a few campsites and an old fashioned pit toilet, plus a few picnic tables. The circular shoreline trail may be walked in under ten minutes, maybe less than five if you speed walk.

Take note please, as of this writing I was told a storm damaged the float and it has not been repaired. Possibly the park is closed, but I would go see for myself. We drove by in late 2012 and the float was still pulled out. but there were some boats anchored. Go check it out!

Tip: Obviously if you anchored here you would be well protected from the wrath of Rosario Strait, so Doe should be on your list of places to run and hide in a pinch.

Sucia Island State Park

Echo Bay, Fossil Bay, Shallow Bay, Fox Cove, Ewing Cove, Snoring Bay

By now you may have noticed that Islands and destinations are being grouped according to general area. The North or Sucia area group is big and has more destinations than you can properly do justice to in one visit or even two cruises. Some people will make this area their destination for a week long cruise and not go to anywhere else. Others like me will stop by one or two spots, spend a night or two and move on. Kayaks are useful all over the San Juans, but at Sucia you will be in kayak paradise.

Tip : Try to get to Sucia early, then you will have time to look around before settling down for the night, or just plan to move the boat the next day, after you have done some exploring.

Tip: To make a reservation for the campgrounds on shore, contact the Sucia Island State Park ranger directly by phone, not the online systems. Call the ranger at (360) 376-2073.

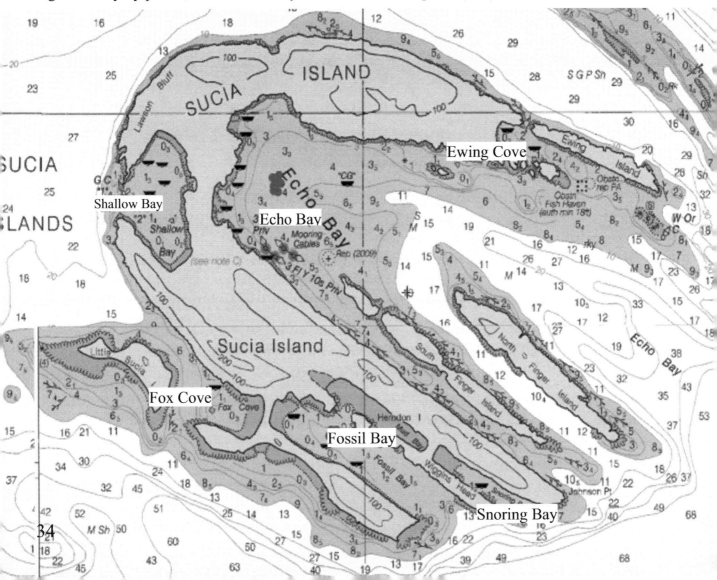

Fossil Bay

Sucia Island

When you first arrive at Sucia you should go straight to Fossil Bay if you want a place at the dock as so many first mates prefer. If there is no room at the inn when you arrive simply anchor nearby (very close) or hook an anchor buoy and wait for someone to depart. There is room at the two floats for many boats so there is a lot of coming and going. You might even consider swinging over in the dinghy and asking around that way you can be ready to swoop in when a space opens up. On a busy weekend there will be others thinking exactly as you, so you need to be ready to scramble. Late in the afternoon spots will open up as day boaters head for home with the last couple hours of daylight.

Once secure at Fossil Bay, you will likely want to dinghy to shore, but you must pick your spot carefully because as the tide drops mud and soft bottom is exposed and you may wish you were at the dock. I suggest bringing the dinghy to the floats and tying up and not have any mud issues at all. You can always make room for another dinghy, just tie to someone else's and be on your way, they will simply retie yours when they return. At least that is the way it is supposed to work with good dinghy dock ettiquette.

At the head of the bay is where most, not all, of the onshore campsites are located, water is up the trail at the top of the gangplank as are the bathrooms. Hiking trails and roads connect all the bays and coves The hike from Ewing Cove to Snoring Bay with a stop at China Caves is a nice long adventure, so bring a lunch and water. Tip: If you have extra people and kayaks or dinghys consider hiking and paddling to a meeting point, then switching off for the return after lunch.

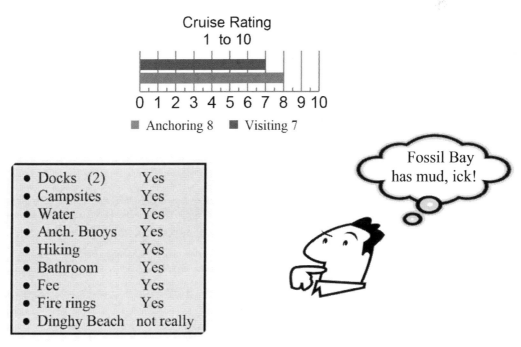

Cruise Rating
1 to 10

0 1 2 3 4 5 6 7 8 9 10

■ Anchoring 8   ■ Visiting 7

● Docks (2)	Yes
● Campsites	Yes
● Water	Yes
● Anch. Buoys	Yes
● Hiking	Yes
● Bathroom	Yes
● Fee	Yes
● Fire rings	Yes
● Dinghy Beach	not really

Fossil Bay has mud, ick!

Fossil Bay

This is where the floats are, two of them and both pretty big., according to the parks dept. 640 feet and 16 buoys (see on the far left almost off the picture) Even though they can hold a lot of boats, don't count on there being room when you arrive, this place gets busy. Out several hundred feet or more are the anchor buoys and lots of room for free anchoring. Just anchor and move over to a dock when someone leaves. Fossil Bay is also where an onshore campground is located. (Behind the camera) Don't let the beach put you off, just tie the dinghy to one of the floats and and walk the service road/trail.

Fox Cove - Snoring Bay - Ewing Cove

Fox Cove is not really a cove, more like a shallow spot between two islands, but people anchor or use one of four buoys. The current will keep the boat pointed one way then the other. The isthmus that separates Fox Cove from Fossil Bay is so narrow you could throw a rock across it, but campers may object. Getting to shore in Fox Cove may be less fun since the beach is kinda rocky as the picture below suggests. The mushroom rock was used a survey marker in the early days.

Snoring Cove has a great name and suggests it may be a good place to rest awhile, but I suspect there could be any number of reasons for the name.

Ewing Bay has four buoys and Snoring Cove has two, I'm combining these two and not saying anything because they are both just quiet places to anchor away from all the hustle of Echo Bay and Fossil Bay. Both have camping areas and bathrooms. The on shore trails are a little bit of a walk from one to the other but easy strolling and mostly level.

China Caves at Shallow Bay Sucia Island

If you have children or are into caves yourself don't miss China Caves at Shallow Bay. China Caves is a sandstone cliff that is eroded away leaving big and little holes pock marking the cliff from ground level all the way up a fifty foot plus cliff.

I was first told about China Caves by our Boy Scout. He was so excited after a sailing visit with his troop that we came back to Sucia a year later just to have him show us China Caves. Legend has it that back in the wild west days the ledges and holes were used to smuggle things and hide people. Some of the caves are quite high up on the cliff face and a fall could be very bad. The cliff is easy to climb which makes it very dangerous so be careful.

I can't give you specifics to find the caves, and there aren't any signs but I will describe how you may find them on your own. The caves are at Shallow Bay and they are at about the middle of the shoreline. Shallow Bay has low forest and low bank access at each end of the 1/3 mile long bay. Near the middle is a cliff that you must go around. That cliff houses China Caves on one side partially hidden by large trees. The shore side trail takes you along the cliff top directly above the caves but you won't know it. Past the cliffs is a steep gully with a nice trail that leads you down to the campground. The caves are in the cliff wall behind the campground, but you need to go look for them, they aren't very obvious. As soon as your crew disappears and sticks their hand our head out a hole yelling look up here, you will know you found them.

Have fun at China Caves and bring your camera. Be safe and be prepared to stop your children from climbing to the top, it's just too easy to resist.

Tip: Anchor in Echo Bay and walk across the narrow isthmus, Shallow Bay has a useless dinghy beach at anything but high tide.

Shallow Bay — Sucia Island

Cruise Rating
1 to 10

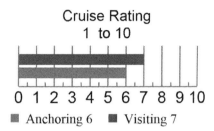

0 1 2 3 4 5 6 7 8 9 10

■ Anchoring 6   ■ Visiting 7

• Dock	No
• Campsites	Yes
• Water	No
• Anch. Buoys	Yes
• Hiking	Yes
• Bathroom	Yes
• Fee	Yes
• Fire rings	Yes
• Dinghy Beach	Yes

Tip: This is a place you can visit on a hike, I see no reason to anchor and certainly not get in my dinghy for a shore trip

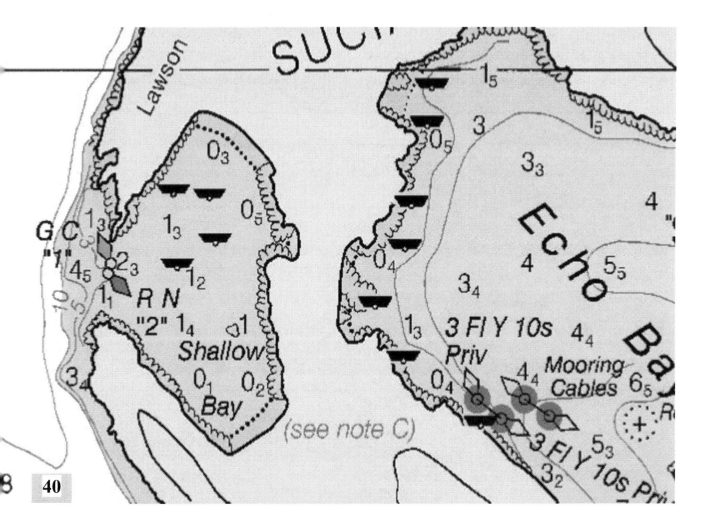

The problem with Shallow Bay is, #1 the beach is so flat your dinghy will get stranded a long way from the water, #2 most of the beach is muck, #3 swells from Boundary Pass freighter traffic will get you in the night.

I recommend you visit by walking from Echo Bay, it's only five minutes or less across the isthmus.

The picture above is the water view of China Caves, the caves are in the trees behind the driftwood pile, the camping area is also behind the driftwood as is the trail down the bank.

Tip: Don't miss China Caves at Shallow Bay, just leave your yacht somewhere else.

Echo Bay

Sucia Island

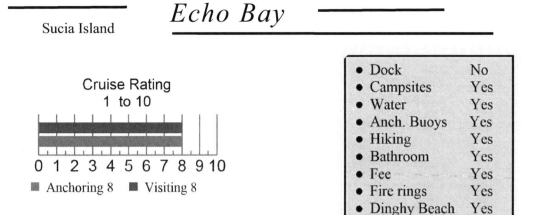

Cruise Rating
1 to 10

0 1 2 3 4 5 6 7 8 9 10

■ Anchoring 8 ■ Visiting 8

- Dock   No
- Campsites   Yes
- Water   Yes
- Anch. Buoys   Yes
- Hiking   Yes
- Bathroom   Yes
- Fee   Yes
- Fire rings   Yes
- Dinghy Beach   Yes

Echo Bay is endless! You arrive and then still have ten minutes before you get there.

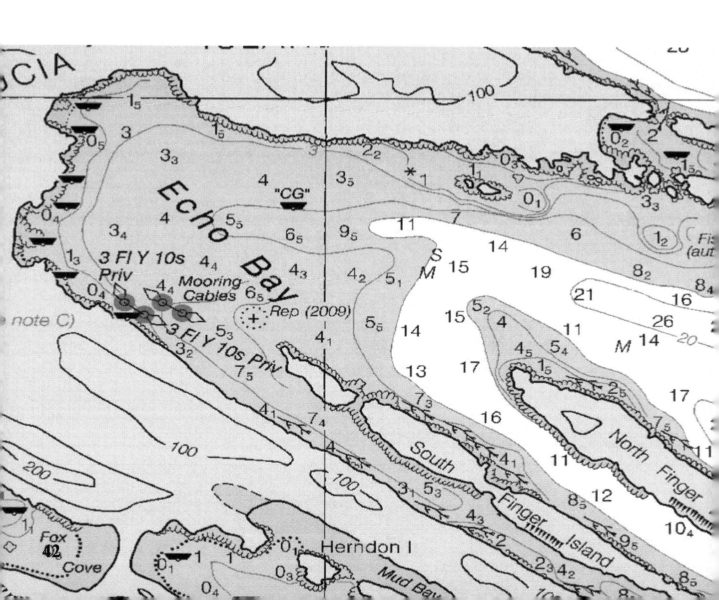

42

Echo Bay

Y ou can't moor close to the north shore like the charts show due to eel grass protection. The buoys and open anchoring area are far enough away that a motorized dinghy is really appreciated. This is where the biggest yachts hang on their anchors. North and South Finger Island are private, but their simple undeveloped presence adds to the parks mystique. No docks to fight over at Echo Bay but they do have a weird lineal mooring buoy, which is just a huge rope stretched taught between floating anchor posts. On shore at the top of the bay are nice composting bathrooms and right off the beach are party size fire rings for group campfires. Unlike Fossil and Shallow Bays the beach is dinghy friendly at most tides which is why I give Echo Bay my thumbs up. We also enjoy the central location for making quick hikes and back to the boat easy. Tip: For you kayakers and dinghy sailors, this is the place to go.

Eel grass protection keeps the boats out a little bit at Echo Bay

Lineal tie ups at Echo Bay are higher than some boats

Echo Bay is great for Dinghy Sailing

West Beach Resort

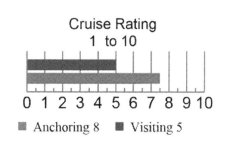

Orcas Island

● Dock	Yes
● Campsites	No
● Water	Yes
● Anch. Buoys	Yes
● Hiking	No
● Bathroom	Yes
● Fee	Yes
● Fire rings	No
● Dinghy Beach	Yes
● Fuel	Yes
● Store	Yes

**Cruise Rating
1 to 10**

0 1 2 3 4 5 6 7 8 9 10

■ Anchoring 8   ■ Visiting 5

West Beach Resort is just where you want a gas stop and deli. When taking the north route around Orcas Island, its location is ideal for the proverbial pit stop. Watch it at low tide the depth gets down around five feet near the gas float. At the top of the ramp is a small store with all the camp type stuff you need. They rent dock space, anchor buoys, and cabins plus have a boat ramp. Tip: This would be another good place to arrange a rendezvous with car travelers or bicyclists. Most importantly, West Beach is where you run for ice when camped at Sucia.

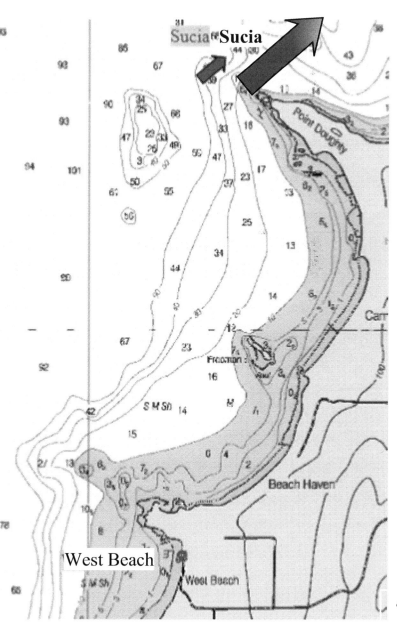

Patos Island State Park

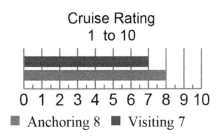

Cruise Rating
1 to 10

0 1 2 3 4 5 6 7 8 9 10

■ Anchoring 8 ■ Visiting 7

● Dock	No
● Campsites	Yes
● Water	No
● Anch. Buoys	Yes
● Hiking	Yes
● Bathroom	Yes
● Fee	Yes
● Fire rings	Yes
● Dinghy Beach	Yes

Y ou have to go to Patos, if for no other reason than its the most northern spot before you get into Canadian waters. There's no float but the bay (not really a bay) for anchoring is snug and mostly protected. Two anchor buoys may or may not be open. You will have a short dinghy trip to an easy to use gravel beach. Patos is north of Sucia and many boaters quit at Echo Bay so there will be a lot less traffic, however its not all that big so your visit could go from loneliness to crowds on the same day. You will be dealing with Georgia Strait currents out at Patos, (not much in the bay) but around the area. Doing a little currents and tides homework may save you some time and fuel. Tip: Read the last sentence again!

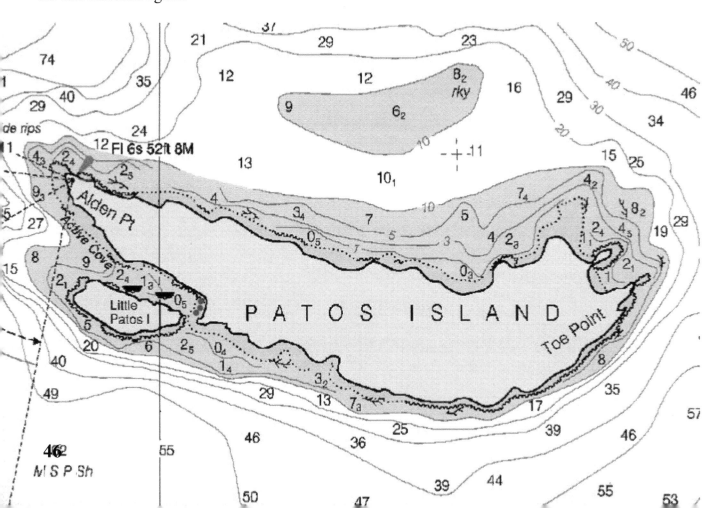

Parks dept. boat with supplys for campground

It is just a ten minute walk out to the automated lighthouse through a mostly open forested setting. Plus you can hike a one mile trail loop. On shore is a small handful of the usual tables, campsites, firepits and bathroom. The shallow little channel between Patos and Little Patos is enticing but is best left to dinghies during slack water.

47

Matia Island State Park

Rating
1 to 10

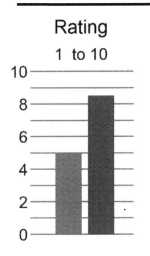

■ Anchoring 5
■ Visiting 8.5

● Dock	No
● Campsites	Yes
● Water	No
● Anch. Buoys	Yes
● Hiking	Yes
● Bathroom	Yes
● Fee	Yes
● Fire rings	No
● Dinghy Beach	Yes

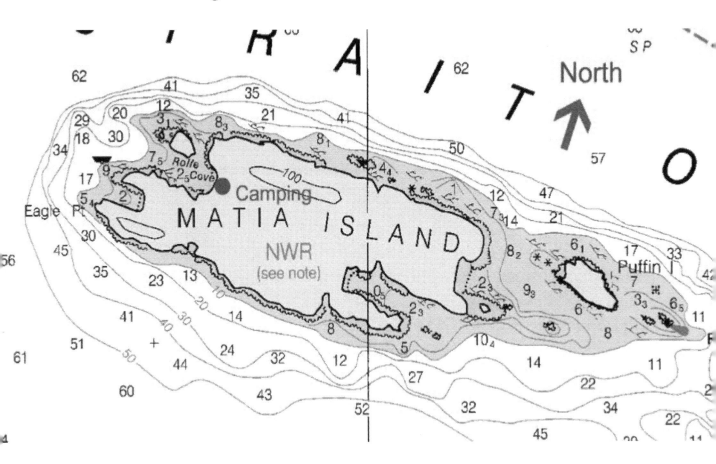

Matia is a close runner up for my favorite place. Matia and Jones are the two places we have hung out for extra days simply because we were enjoying ourselves so much. Rolfe Cove at Matia, is small and has a current at the float that adds to the fun but don't let that dissuade you, there are currents everywhere. (Almost) The float is a small one holding only four medium size boats. On shore are two or three campsites and the standard composters. A few years ago they took out the firepits and made all of Matia campfire free. It was devastating news, but we got over it. Out in the cove are two anchor buoys, plus just a little bit of room close to the gravel beach to anchor a few more boats. At the other end of the island is a very protected cove with a view of Lummi Island where you will find easy anchoring and solitude. Tip: On shore at Matia is probably why we keep going back, there is an outstanding rain forest and shoreline trail unlike any other in the San Juans. We will go to Matia first and if there is no room at the float or buoy, we run to Sucia where there is endless room, then come back to Matia later to try again.

Eagles and Puffins are common entertainers providing just the right amount of diversion. Kayakers paddle over from East Sound for overnighters.

If you anchor at the east end of Matia, simply dinghy to shore at the head of the cove to locate the trail. Without fire pits, I can't rate a 10 anymore.

Matia Island offers her all and promises nothing, but I think it would be impossible to stop by for a while and not be better for it.

Matia

Minus tide at Matia Float - Easy strolling trail below

Matia Island

" *A good day cruising is better than a good day working*"

Cypress Island

Cypress Head
Eagle Harbor
Pelican Beach

Cypress Head and Pelican Beach are popular destinations for kayakers and small sailboats from Anacortes and Bellingham. For them, visiting Cypress does not require crossing Rosario Strait. You don't need to cross Rosario either to get to the best hiking and beachfront camping around.

Cypress is DNR property (Dept. of Nat. Resources) and so for some odd reason they don't charge a fee, and there is no fee box. But donations are accepted by a local group from the mainland that keeps the places looking good.

If you came to the San Juans to hike, boat, sail, and camp, look no further. Rosario Strait on one side and Bellingham Bay on the other satisfies sailing to the max. Eagle Bluff and Smugglers Cove are perfect hikes. Camping, whether you sleep on shore or in the boat is top notch at Pelican Beach and Cypress Head. If they had docks and ice machines it would be nice, but not any better.

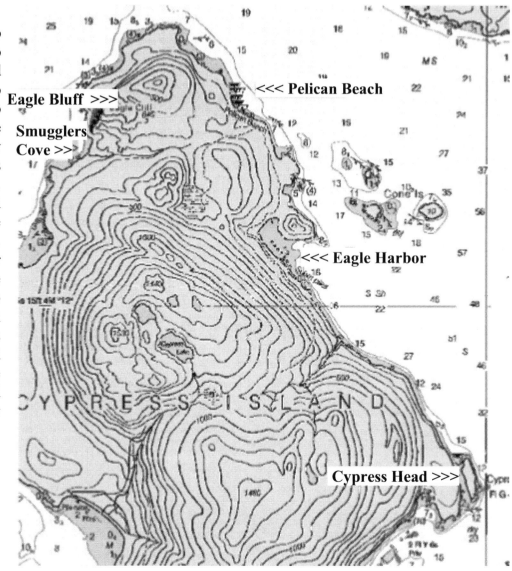

Cypress Head

Cypress Head is actually a tiny island next to Cypress Island and connected with a narrow isthmus where you land your dinghy. No floats, but in the little bay are three anchor buoys. If you can get your boat in close enough you can get out of the swells and wakes that sometime plague boaters at unprotected Pelican Beach a short distance northward. On shore are campsites with the best views and even worse falls if you sleep walk.

Trails from the beach connect with the rest of Cypress Island trails, linking to Pelican Beach, Eagle Harbor, and Eagle Bluff.

- Dock   No
- Campsites   Yes
- Water   No
- Anch. Buoys   Yes
- Hiking   Yes
- Bathroom   Yes
- Fee   No
- Fire rings   Yes
- Dinghy Beach   Yes

Cruise Rating
1 to 10

0 1 2 3 4 5 6 7 8 9 10

■ Anchoring 6   ■ Visiting 8.5

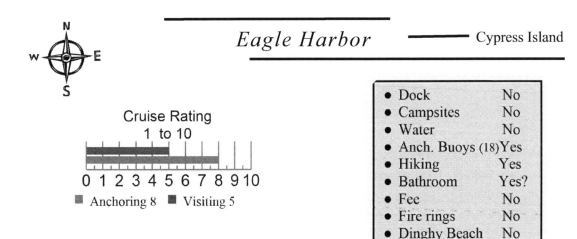

Eagle Harbor ——— Cypress Island

Cruise Rating
1 to 10

0 1 2 3 4 5 6 7 8 9 10

■ Anchoring 8   ■ Visiting 5

- Dock   No
- Campsites   No
- Water   No
- Anch. Buoys (18) Yes
- Hiking   Yes
- Bathroom   Yes?
- Fee   No
- Fire rings   No
- Dinghy Beach No

Some places jump out at you offering wonderful amenities, the total is greater than the parts. Its not true at Eagle Harbor, the total package is less, and here is why. The dinghy beach is sub par. The protected cove is wonderful for anchoring and 18 plus buoys are hard to argue with, but the water is shallow , full of grass, and the shore is mostly mushy. The bathrooms are hidden in the woods and getting to them by dinghy is trying to say the least, even a losing battle for some. I will not rank Eagle Harbor less because I got to shore and so can you. Plus I found a gravel dinghy beach near the south edge that was usable so getting on to the trail system worked. Its no wonder no one has campfires or gets off their boats. I will probably come back, but only to anchor or hook a buoy.

In all fairness though, it is hard to measure up when sandwiched between neighbors like Pelican Beach and Cypress Head.

I just remembered its free, now I feel bad. I should add a couple points.

Lets see that's
18 points for 18 buoys
Minus 24 for no fire pits
Less 10 for bad beach
Plus 21 for being free
makes 5

Pelican Beach

Cypress Island

Cruise Rating
1 to 10

0 1 2 3 4 5 6 7 8 9 10

■ Anchoring 7 ■ Visiting 9

• Dock	No
• Campsites	Yes
• Water	No
• Anch. Buoys	Yes
• Hiking	Yes
• Bathroom	Yes
• Fee	No
• Fire rings	Yes
• Dinghy Beach	Yes

"There are only a few cherished places where great memories become etched into ones psyche."

I magine! A beach with nothing but skipping stones, a warm campfire and plentiful driftwood. Your boat anchored peacefully only 50 yds away.

Imagine! Hiking to Smugglers Cove.

Imagine! The view from Eagle Bluff.

Tip: This place is well liked for good reason.

55

- Dock   No
- Campsites   Yes
- Water   No
- Anch. Buoys   Yes
- Hiking   Yes
- Bathroom   Yes
- Fee   Yes
- Fire rings   Yes
- Dinghy Beach Yes

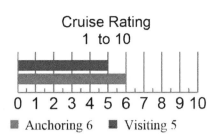

Cruise Rating
1 to 10

0 1 2 3 4 5 6 7 8 9 10

■ Anchoring 6   ■ Visiting 5

Clark is another of the drive by Islands on the way to somewhere else. My recommendation for Clark is to stop by for a quick lunch, walk around the island for thirty minutes, skip a few stones and then move on. Clark is low, narrow and small, but does have a restroom, nice campsites, and anchor buoys. Otherwise, really not much going for it unless you need a place to camp or anchor and its getting dark.

It's not much more than a speed bump in Rosario Strait which means wind and waves when the weather kicks up. I wouldn't want to be stuck on Clark in a storm. It's depressing just thinking about it. Being in the middle of the strait makes for an unrelenting back and forth current that will snatch away anything loose. On the plus side Clark offers great dinghy beaches and awesome sunsets. Tip: stay clear of the Sisters, and the underwater hook forming the anchoring bay.

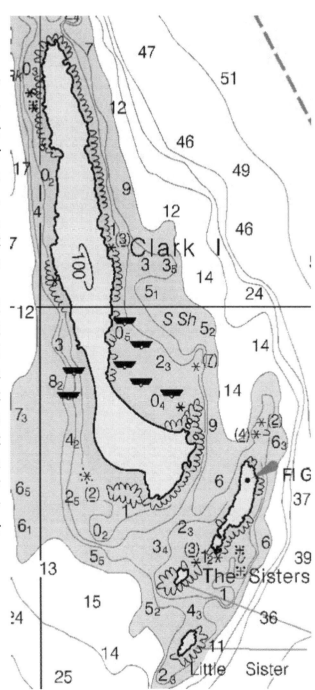

James Island State Park

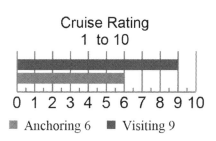

Cruise Rating
1 to 10

0 1 2 3 4 5 6 7 8 9 10

■ Anchoring 6   ■ Visiting 9

• Dock	Yes
• Campsites	Yes
• Water	No
• Anch. Buoys	Yes
• Hiking	Yes
• Bathroom	Yes
• Fee	Yes
• Fire rings	Yes
• Dinghy Beach	Yes

If you wanted to make the claim of Sentinel to the San Juans, you could arguably give little James Island the title and then herald nearby Thatcher Pass as "Entrance to the San Juans." The chart below below shows how close James is to Thatcher Pass the main thoroughfare for those heading to the San Juans from Anacortes.

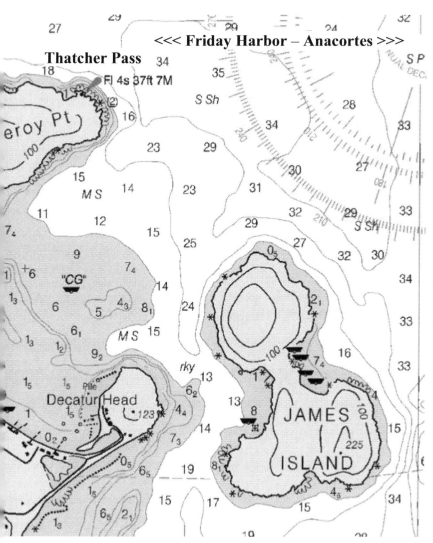

Just like many San Juan Islands, James is all park with no inhabitants or private lands, its distinctive dog bone shape creates two bays. The west bay is well protected, although sometimes currents will swing you at anchor. The east side is open to the wrath of Rosario.

James has a smallish four boat float and wharf in the western bay and five or so anchor buoys on the east side. The beaches are dinghy friendly at all tide levels. On shore are three separate campgrounds, one designated just for kayaks. The sign says human powered vessels, but canoes and rowboats are simply not seen so kayaks is what they really mean. Fire pits, picnic tables, compost toilets, great shoreline and over the top hiking trails complete this very nice island park.

The narrow isthmus gives you a front row seat from the campground picnic area to view conditions in Rosario Strait. If you are lucky, you may see passing Orca Pods when they swim by like we did once at 7am.

57

Inati Bay

Lummi Island

• Dock	No
• Campsites	No
• Water	No
• Anch. Buoys	No
• Hiking	No
• Bathroom	No
• Fee	No
• Fire rings	No
• Dinghy Beach	Yes

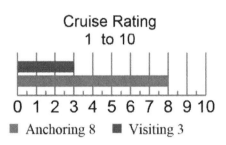

Cruise Rating
1 to 10

0 1 2 3 4 5 6 7 8 9 10

■ Anchoring 8   ■ Visiting 3

Inati Bay on the east side of Lummi Island offers a place to run and seek refuge in a blow or just a picturesque spot to drop the hook for lunch. On shore is private forest land, but its ok to stroll the short gravel beach. There are no structures or homes to spoil the view so you will feel quite secluded and private. The bay offers good protection for half a dozen+ boats but you will likely be alone. This is a good protected spot to stop for the night or swing in for a sail change when Bellingham Bay gets out of hand. It would be a good destination if you got a late start out of Squalicum Harbor or nightfall catches you .

Tip: Mark your chart so you don't forget where Inati is. When things get snotty its nice to have a mouse hole. (South East side of Lummi)

Smugglers cove to the north has houses on shore, so its not private at all.

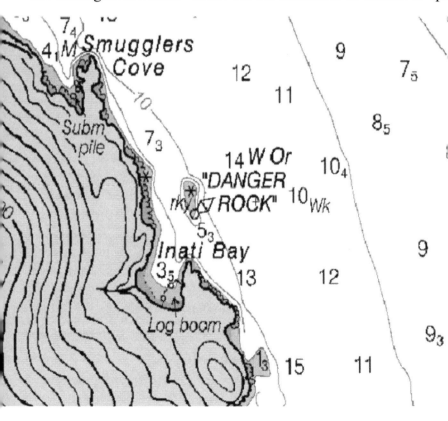

Squalicum Harbor

Bellingham

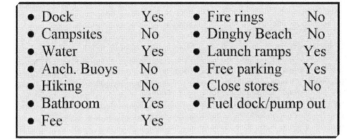

• Dock	Yes	• Fire rings	No
• Campsites	No	• Dinghy Beach	No
• Water	Yes	• Launch ramps	Yes
• Anch. Buoys	No	• Free parking	Yes
• Hiking	No	• Close stores	No
• Bathroom	Yes	• Fuel dock/pump out	
• Fee	Yes		

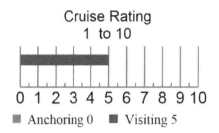

Cruise Rating
1 to 10

0 1 2 3 4 5 6 7 8 9 10

■ Anchoring 0   ■ Visiting 5

Squalicum Harbor in Bellingham is by far the best ramp and facility around and has my highest recommendation. If your planning to go to Sucia for the first night, Squalicum Harbor is the closest launching place. Four lanes, suitable at all tide levels, open 24/7.   Loads of *free parking,* long or short term (this is a $100+ savings).   Fresh water wash down hoses. Tip: always wash your trailer immediately after immersion, don't wait until you return a week later. On site restaurants, bathrooms with showers, and transient docks for overnight visits complete this close to perfect package. Major stores are near, but not walking distance. Fuel dock & pump out are at hand as well. If you prefer to sling your boat they have travel lifts available, you will need to call and reserve a launching date.

Bellingham is much bigger than Anacortes, and Squalicum Harbor is easily twice the size of Cap Sante with two boat basins side by side. When driving your rig up the freeway you may be thinking that Anacortes is closest and fastest to get in the water and you would be mostly correct, but its not much further or longer to Squalicum because you have freeway the entire way.

I am a big fan of ramp launching, mostly because it saves a ton of boat dollars but also because our cruises include the entire time away from home, not just the time on the boat. We have found that when we take our time driving, making sure to stop along the way to smell the flowers, getting things done in our own fastidious stubborn way, launching on *our schedule,* casting off when *we are ready*, and not setting ourselves up for problems, is the basis for having a relaxing enjoyable outing. *Tip: take it easy, go slow.*

Tip: Bellingham boasts a Farmers Market that is just a one mile walk from Squalicum Harbor at Depot Market Square, Railroad and Chestnut streets, open 10am to 3pm April thru Christmas.

Cap Sante

Anacortes

• Dock	Yes		• Fire rings	No	
• Campsites	No		• Dinghy Beach	No	
• Water	Yes		• Launch Ramp	No	
• Anch. Buoys	No		• Long term pkg	Yes	
• Hiking	No		• Travel lift/sling	Yes	
• Bathroom	Yes		• Fuel - pump out	Yes	
• Fee	Yes		• Stores	Yes	

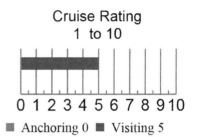

Cruise Rating
1 to 10

0 1 2 3 4 5 6 7 8 9 10

■ Anchoring 0   ■ Visiting 5

Cap Sante is the premium starting point for many going to the San Juans, unfortunately they don't have a launching ramp, only travel lifts and slings. Keeping your trailer salt free is always a good thing, but somehow you have to get your boat in the water so trade offs must be made. I recommend that you call in advance to reserve your launch window and don't rely on what your told to plan your trip. We have been disappointed so many times at boat yards that we have learned to avoid them. The problem is that their schedule is not your schedule and you will get bumped. When making plans with any yard do not expect to get in the water and make any late in the day dashes across the strait to your destination. Give yourself the entire day, start early, be flexible and hope for the best. On your return do the same. It may be easiest to plan to stay at the marina your first and last nights This scheduling issue is one of the reasons we prefer to use ramps. Ramps are 24/7 and you are in charge. I'm not condemning Cap Sante, I have used all their services quite satisfactorily, I'm condemning boat yards in general.

Cap Sante is across the street from a Safeway store and just a short walk to West Marine. Part of the facility is a large RV parking area where you can stay on your boat on the trailer or you can pay just for trailer parking and take off for distant shores as soon as your in the water.

The marina has plenty of transient slips available and nice bathrooms and showers. Anacortes itself is an interesting city with lots of good restaurants to enjoy. La Conner and Deception Pass are less than thirty minute drives and it makes good sense to visit them by car if your cruise doesn't include them, which gives you something to do if you stay at the marina your first and last nights.

Tip: Think outside the boat, your car can cover a lot of destinations while your boat provides a welcome berth when you get back.

Tip: Local knowledge, The bowling alley used to have a great cafe inside, and the Anacortes Farmers market is at 611 R Ave in Anacortes, just a few steps from Cap Sante Boat Haven, and runs 9am until closing every Saturday beginning in May.

Washington Park

Anacortes City Park

Cruise Rating
1 to 10

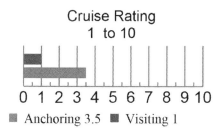

0 1 2 3 4 5 6 7 8 9 10

■ Anchoring 3.5 ■ Visiting 1

● Dock	Yes
● Campsites	Yes
● Water	Yes
● Anch. Buoys	No
● Hiking	Yes
● Bathroom	Yes
● Fee	Yes
● Fire rings	Yes
● Dinghy Beach	Yes

Washington Park in Anacortes

City park (campground) with ramp. This is your #1 choice for car camping with a boat. You can go out for day trips, and then keep the boat on the trailer at your camp site. Or splash the boat and take off for a week or more. Parking fee used to be $8 day. Calling for campground reservations is a must. The boat launch parking area gets full on week ends and there is no overflow area. The city map below shows Cap Sante and Washington Park. (red dots) Constant vessel traffic make sleeping at anchor nauseous. You can use the ramp without camping or vice versa. This is the closest jump off point to Friday Harbor, and just three miles across Rosario Strait to James Island. Tip: don't ignore or discount this place.

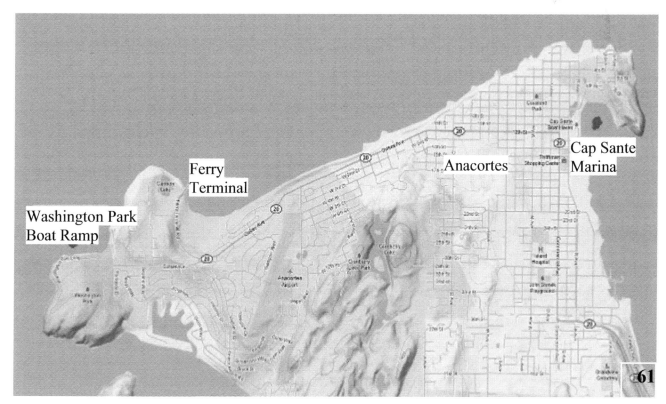

Ferry Terminal

Anacortes

Cap Sante Marina

Washington Park Boat Ramp

Saddlebag Island State Park

Cruise Rating
1 to 10

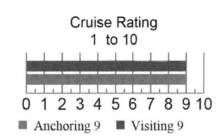

0 1 2 3 4 5 6 7 8 9 10

■ Anchoring 9 ■ Visiting 9

● Dock	No
● Campsites	Yes
● Water	No
● Anch. Buoys	No
● Hiking	Yes
● Bathroom	Yes
● Fee	Yes
● Fire rings	Yes
● Dinghy Beach	Yes

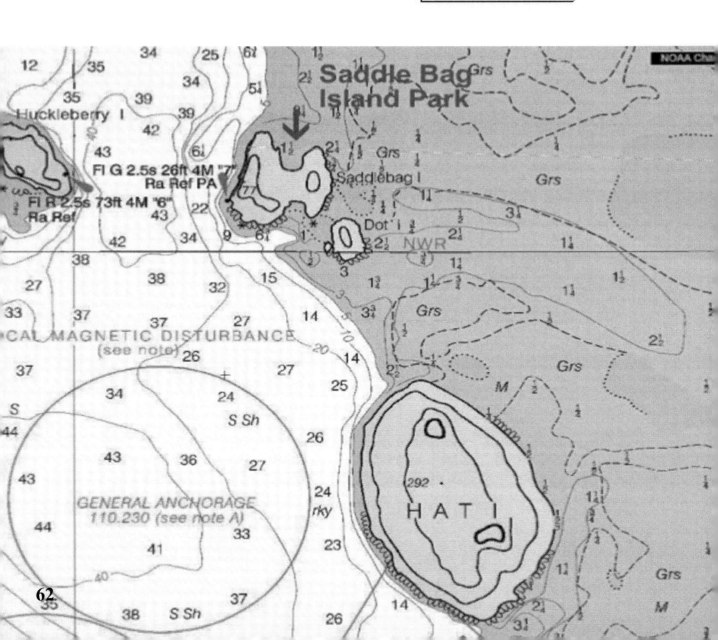

Saddlebag Island is probably the most overlooked of the drive by Islands. It's so close to the mainland that many will simply continue on to Cap Sante or La Conner for the evening. Those boaters just heading out in the morning going the other way may fail to consider its diminutive size as a worthy destination, especially early in the day. Saddlebag offers a welcome refuge in a storm, or when you get caught just an hour before sundown with no place to go. When darkness is descending like clockwork, you will welcome this little jewel of an island. Few cruisers enjoy arriving or navigating in the dark, and the inherent danger darkness brings to cruising is undeniable.

Saddlebag has a small cove with good holding very close to shore. It is slightly off the beaten path, so passing sleep disturbing wakes are infrequent or nonexistent making for a relaxing visit and peaceful dreams.

" The calm waters of Saddlebag's little cove welcome us as the sun begins its final plunge. We have enough time for a hike and then smores around a campfire. Little did we know that our galley sink water pump switch would fail while we were on shore pumping overboard our entire supply of fresh water, and then as a bonus burn out the pump. Luckily we found a bottle of water to make morning coffee."

Tip: throw the main battery switch!

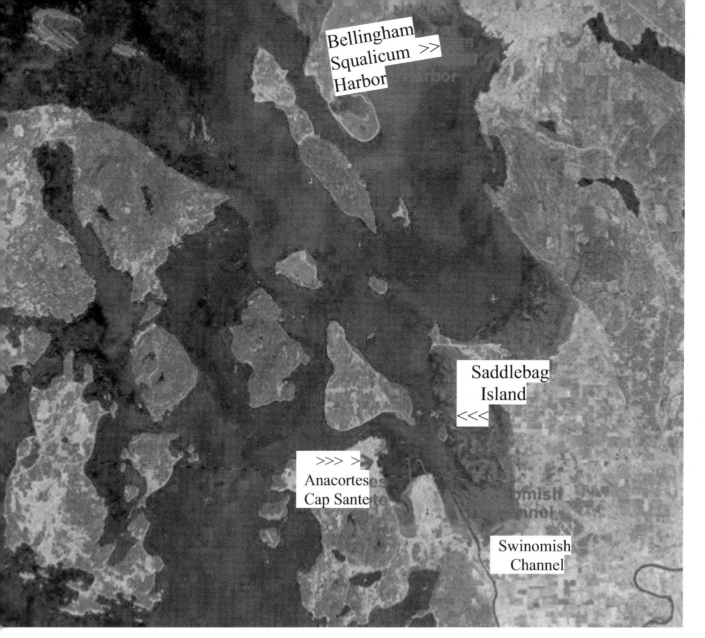

Bellingham
Squalicum >>
Harbor

Saddlebag
Island
<<<

>>> >
Anacortes
Cap Sante

Swinomish
Channel

When you arrive, if the little cove happens to be filled to capacity with two or three boats, don't worry, just anchor a little further out, it won't make any difference. There is no dock at Saddlebag, but the beach is very dinghy friendly or you can beach your runabout or swing keeler. Just don't forget if you plan to beach your yacht, there is nowhere in the San Juans that is unaffected by tide, so bring the necessary gear for beaching and off shore anchoring if you don't bring a dinghy.

On shore at Saddlebag are a dozen or more campsites from beach front to very private, all have fire rings and picnic tables. The place is normally deserted, so whenever you arrive you may have it all to yourself.

Circling the island is an easy to walk shoreline trail that takes about an hour if you stop many times to enjoy the vistas. As a bonus, there are several good overlooks where you can snap pics of your boat in the cove.

Saddlebag Island

You would be correct to assume I give Saddlebag a big thumbs up. We try to arrange for a lunch stop and hike whenever we are going by. One of our most cherished visits was highlighted by sharing hot soup in the boat after we snuggled shivering by a campfire watching the sun set over our boat one cold frosty evening. Our son still talks about how extraordinarily good the soup was that night. Maybe I'll see you there someday, we can share some ramen.

From shore I noticed that the sun had set on all the boats but ours, fittingly named

"Sunshine"

This peaceful picture is an accurate depiction of Saddlebag and cruising the San Juan's, minus the bone chilling cold we felt when leaving the campfire that night.

One of my best decisions that day was to anchor at Saddlebag Island for the evening.   65

La Conner

• Dock	Yes
• Campsites	No
• Water	Yes/No
• Anch. Buoys	No
• Hiking	No
• Bathroom	Yes
• Fee	Yes
• Fuel/pump out	Yes
• Fire rings	No
• Dinghy Beach	No
• Launch Ramp	Yes
• Long term pkg	Yes
• Stores/Restaurants	Yes
• Quaintness/ambience	Yes+

Cruise Rating

1 to 10

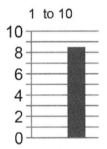

■ Anchoring 0
■ Visiting 8.5

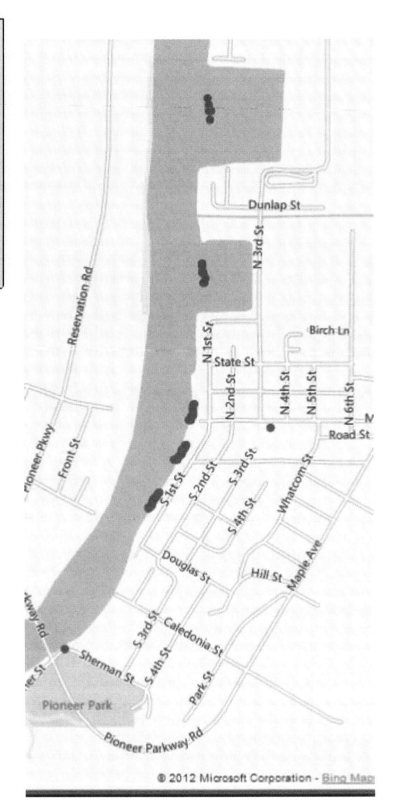

@ 2012 Microsoft Corporation - Bing Map

Imagine vivid bright yellow

La Conner is another one of those secrets that you will be glad you discovered, and the sooner the better. If only someone would have told you years ago. Well now that you know the secret, you need to know where to tie up.

Look over on the left page, the dark waterway is Swinomish channel. Deception Pass and Seattle are south, or off the page, north or off the top is Anacortes.

- The first little dot at the bottom is the single lane city boat ramp and a one or two boat float. Parking is $2-3 day, I forget. We have used the ramp, its good to go at all tides except the very lowest.
- Moving up, the three bars are all city floats for transient boaters.
  (the floats are marked with yellow and are easy to spot) They have pay kiosks.
- The next two bars out in the middle of the bays are the Port of Skagit County transient boater floats. (This is the big marina with fuel and pump outs, and sling hoists, and fee parking lots)
- The little dot inland at 3rd and Morris St. marks Pioneer Grocery, where you can get anything you need, and they are open late.

I'm not going to gush about La Conner, suffice it to say, I recommend you make a point to visit by land or sea. You will be rewarded with shops, galleries and restaurants five minutes or less from the boat. How cool is that?

67

Deception Pass State Park

Cornet Bay - Sharpe Cove - Bowman Bay

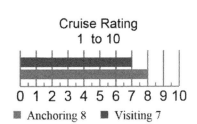

Cruise Rating
1 to 10

0 1 2 3 4 5 6 7 8 9 10

■ Anchoring 8   ■ Visiting 7

• Dock	Yes	• Fee	Yes
• Campsites	Yes	• Fire rings	Yes
• Water	No	• Dinghy Beach	Yes
• Anch. Buoys	Yes	• Launch Ramp	Yes
• Hiking	Yes	• Long Term Pkg	Yes
• Bathroom	Yes		

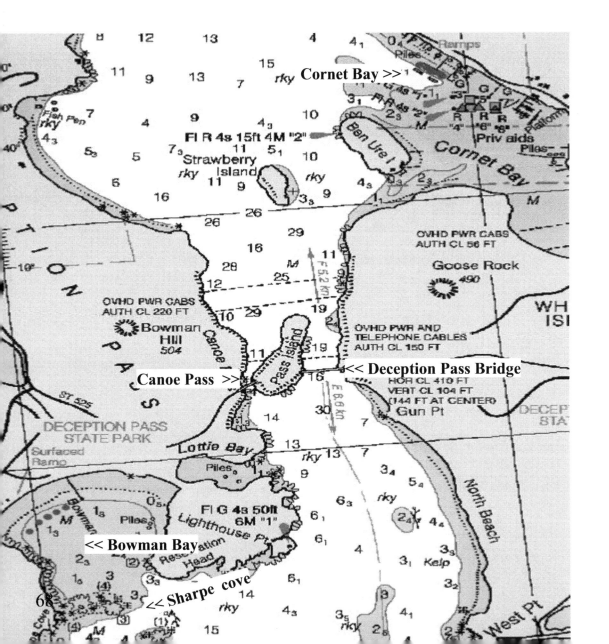

Deception Pass State Park is large and has several campgrounds, islands, and of course the pass itself spanned by a picturesque bridge.

Cornet Bay is the main attraction where overnight floats and launching ramps are located. The floats will hold quite a few boats and we have never failed to find room even when arriving late. To save the fee you can always anchor just a dinghy ride away and there is all the room you could want. Because swarms of people arrive by car, there is always lots of fishing from the floats. It may seem rude (it is in a way) but boats have the right away and you should just park the boat in front of an offending child with a pole and he will move. At the top of the gang plank is a single overused but brand new bathroom, and a water faucet that has never been turned on since installed. The only water you can get is what you can coax out of the bathroom sink.

The local store is well stocked and about a quarter mile walk. Hiking is more like walking on service roads or the highway itself, but there are a few loop trails to the left of the docks up a gated road. We once took the dinghy and crossed the bay where we climbed the bank and found the trail to the bridge. The trail was about fifteen feet into the woods so

Front row seats through Deception Pass are what it's all about

bushwhacking was minimal. The hike to the bridge and then on to the summit ended with a monster view all the way to the San Juan Islands and onto Victoria, and of course the Olympic Mountains for good measure. (Not bad for a foggy beginning that day) Returning to find the dinghy was a bit of a challenge because I neglected to pay attention to where we climbed the bank. Tip: Pay attention to where you leave your toys.

Several times we have stayed multiple days at the floats in Cornet Bay just passing time, and then move over to Sharpe Cove and continue hiking and hanging out. Tip:You could arrange to meet friends that come by car and share good times.

Cornet Bay is where you will want to wait for weather conditions to improve, or perhaps detour through Swimnomish Channel.

Deception Pass & Canoe Pass

Transiting the pass is easy most of the time, but the current may be flowing against you, or a combination of tides, winds, storms may cause some standing waves under the bridge. The tidal changes are roughly every six hours so that means four times a day the water flattens out and then reverses direction. Most sailboats will need to time their passage not to be fighting against maximum ebb or flood, because they may not have enough speed. Maximum flow will only last a short time, a little earlier or a little later (one hour) may make a huge difference.

Motoring with the current is a little like riding down a swift river. The narrowest point is where the current is the swiftest and that is directly under the bridge for about one hundred feet, once past the bridge on either side things slow down quickly. There is lots of room to pass or meet other boats in the pass.

Canoe Pass on the other hand is narrow and you don't want to meet another boat. Deception Pass and Canoe Pass share the little island the bridge sits on in the middle (Pass Island) You can't mistake the two passes, Canoe Pass is not very big, but it is navigable if you are careful and want a thrill. Warning: never approach Canoe Pass riding with the current or you will get sucked into something you can't stop. Always approach Canoe Pass against the current so you can simply look it over

Canoe Pass in Deception Pass Park

before committing to going all the way, or better yet wait for slack water, and then you can circle Pass Island in your dinghy. The cliff walls and bridge make for some spectacular photos, be sure to look up and wave at the people looking down from the bridge.

Launching Ramp: The ramps (four) at Cornet Bay are first rate and may be used at all tide levels 24/7 There is a super size parking lot and with proper payment you can park as long as you need. Tip: This is a good place to begin and end any cruise.

See more on launching ramps in the launching ramp section.

Canoe Pass, has a little S turn so you can't see all the way through. Approach this place with caution

Cornet Bay floats at Deception Pass Park

Cruising rewards!
Meeting new friends in pajamas while fishing on a cruise.
(then actually catching a fish)

Bowman Bay
and Sharpe Cove

Deception Pass State Park

Cruise Rating
1 to 10

0 1 2 3 4 5 6 7 8 9 10

■ Anchoring 5   ■ Visiting 6

• Dock	Yes	• Bathroom	Yes
• Campsites	Yes	• Fee	Yes
• Water	Yes	• Fire rings	Yes
• Anch. Buoys	Yes	• Dinghy Beach	Yes
• Hiking	Yes		

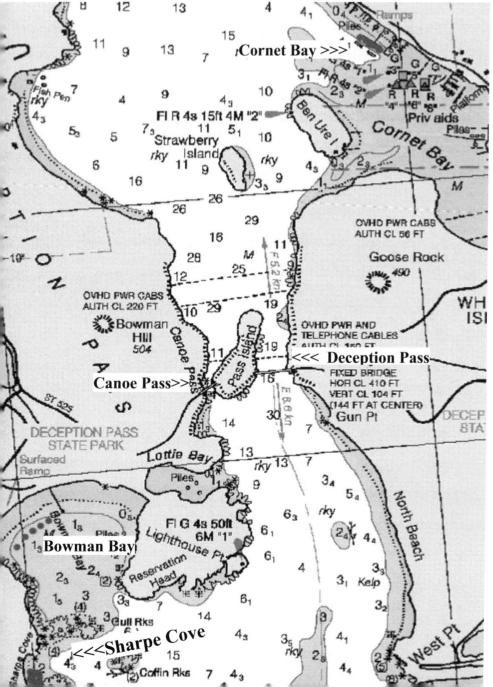

Bowman Bay buoys are marked in dots in the lower left corner.

Cornet Bay docks and launching ramps are in the upper right corner.

Sharpe cove dock is in the bottom left corner.

Deception Pass and Canoe Pass are dead center.

Tip: Canoe Pass is not safe for all boats at all times. Deception Pass may have standing waves at times and requires your caution.

74

Bowman Bay and Sharpe cove are really just a combined semi protected bay with some awash rocks playing spoiler. The rocks are easy to spot and marked on your chart. One small dock that only holds four small boats if your lucky for overnight stays is at Sharpe Cove and over in the Bowman section there are five anchor buoys. There is a fishing pier that is for foot traffic only, no boats may tie up.

On shore at Sharpe Cove are bathrooms and a day use picnic area plus interpretive kiosks including a large wood carving depicting the legend "Maiden of Deception Pass." Sharpe Cove is also your access point to Rosario beach only one hundred feet beyond the gangplank. Rosario Beach is renowned as a tide pool area. Sharpe cove is well worth stopping for thirty minutes, a day, or overnight. You can hike all of Deception Pass rocks and points and even hike up to the bridge and down the other side. Since this is a vehicle accessed park you will have plenty of visitors coming down the walkway asking questions and checking out your boat. Over at the anchor buoys in Bowman Bay you will find you are anchored offshore of one of the parks campgrounds. Your only access to the campground bathrooms will be by dinghy.

This is great place to wait for the tide to change, since the pass is only five minutes away. Its also where you may end up taking refuge from fog if you can't make it back through the pass to Cornet Bay.

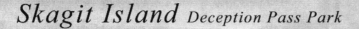

Skagit Island *Deception Pass Park*

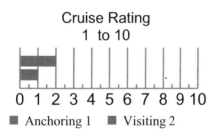

Cruise Rating
1 to 10

0 1 2 3 4 5 6 7 8 9 10

■ Anchoring 1   ■ Visiting 2

- Dock   No
- Campsites   Yes
- Water   No
- Anch. Buoys   Yes
- Hiking   Yes
- Bathroom   Yes
- Fee   Yes
- Fire rings   Yes
- Dinghy Beach Yes
- Safe – not really!

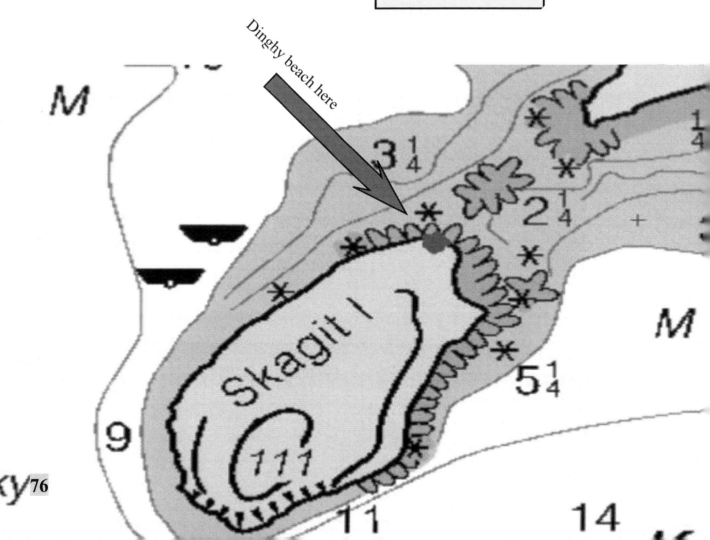

Dinghy beach here

M

3 1/4

1/4

2 1/4

+

M

Skagit I

5 1/4

9

777

11

14

Skagit is part of Deception Pass Park, but really is more suitable for kayakers than cruisers. The above picture is of the one and only campsite complete with pay station.

The single anchor buoy is subject to wakes and swells and I wouldn't trust it staying put. Anchoring near the small dinghy beach subjects the boat to swift currents between Skagit and nearby Kiket Island. The perimeter trail is not safe due to dangerous cliffs inches from trail edge and hidden by overhanging salal bushes.

The views from the trail are outstanding and it's close proximity to Cornet Bay makes it an easy paddle, if that's where you put in.

It is difficult to write a scathing review when I really did enjoy my one visit and intend to return, but I don't want anyone to think this is an easy place to get to, or a walk in the park once there.

If you are addicted to gunk holing, as some of us certainly are, then problem currents, kelp, rocks, cliffs, and so forth are simply issues to resolve while exploring cool places. Skagit is one of those cool yet nasty places.

Tip: Plan your thirty minute visit for slack tide, that will ease the suffering.

Hope Island

Deception Pass State Park

Cruise Rating
1 to 10

0 1 2 3 4 5 6 7 8 9 10

■ Anchoring 5   ■ Visiting 2

- Dock   No
- Campsites   Yes
- Water   No
- Anch. Buoys   Yes
- Hiking   No
- Bathroom   Yes
- Fee   Yes
- Fire rings   Yes
- Dinghy Beach   Yes

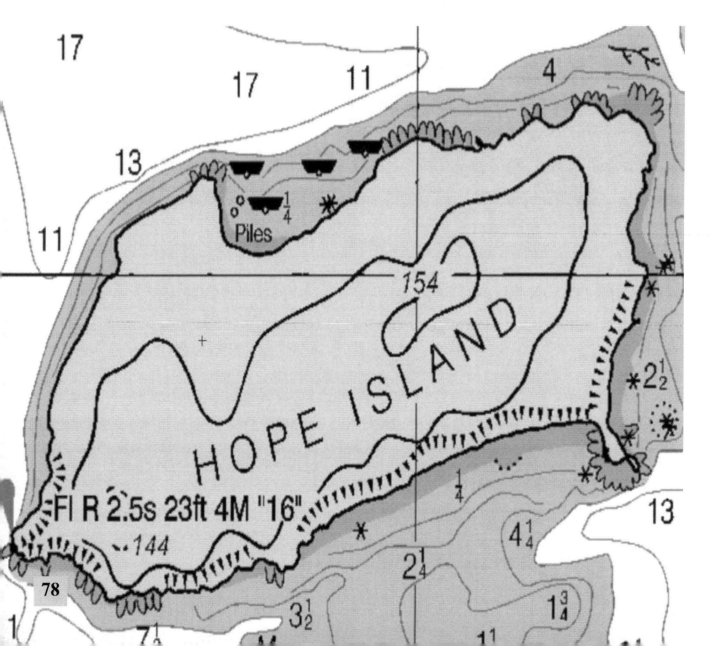

Hope Island is part of Deception Pass State Park and is located in the north end of Skagit Bay. You will drive by Hope on your way to and from Swinomish Channel. The anchorage with just a few buoys is protected from passing boat wakes by a little hook of land. There is easy anchoring with plenty of room near the buoys or further around the back side. Furthermost in at the head of the cove is a little gravel dinghy beach providing access to three campsites, an outhouse, picnic tables, and some fire rings sums it up. There are no trails to speak of and heavy forest will dissuade any bushwhacking. Being only 2 ½ miles from busy and sometimes crowded Cornet Bay makes Hope a good choice for some peace and quiet, or while waiting a current change in the pass.

A positive point for Hope Island is that it is not out of your way, so you may as well check it out on your way from Deception Pass to La Conner.

As a place to anchor, Hope rates a 5

but as a place to visit only a 2

Bowman Bay from campground
See the anchor buoys? (me neither?)

Fort Whitman

on Goat Island

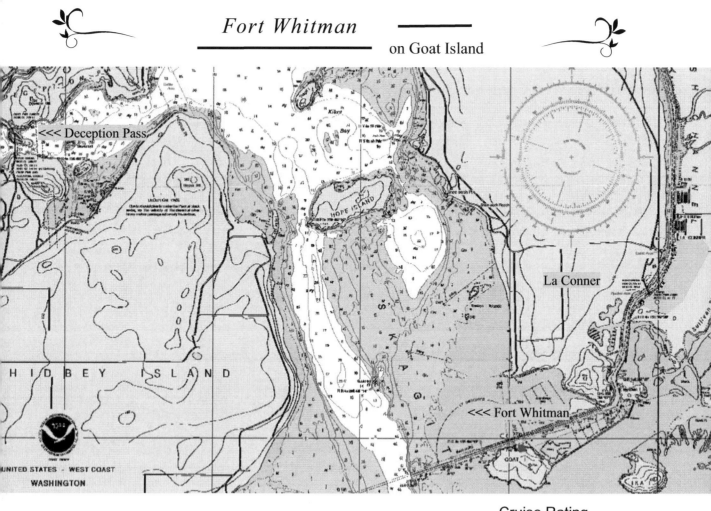

<<< Deception Pass

La Conner

<<< Fort Whitman

HIDBEY ISLAND

UNITED STATES - WEST COAST
WASHINGTON

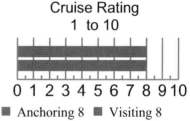

Cruise Rating
1 to 10

0 1 2 3 4 5 6 7 8 9 10

■ Anchoring 8   ■ Visiting 8

Sometimes it pays to read the fine print on your chart. It certainly did the day Linda said, "What's this Fort Whitman here?" The pictures on the next page tell it all.

This is how you get there. Find Goat Island at the very southern end of Swinomish Channel just before it dumps you into Skagit Bay. You can't miss it. While skirting Goat Island (stay in channel) and dodging the ever present log rafts, be looking for the group of pilings for the old wharf. They are the only pilings with a *row of rusty metal brackets up at the tops*. Anchor near the wharf pilings and run your dinghy ashore directly opposite them. Look for a trail that leads to the right or bushwhack *to the the right* while you climb up hill. About 100 yards up the hill to the right is the old gun emplacement completely overgrown and invisible from the water.

You can anchor and pay the 1909 battery a visit and be back on the boat in one hour, or you can spend the day hiking trails and discover the range bunkers and other structures out on the west point of the island. No camping here, just a day hike.

80

Fort Whitman and Battery Harrison were built to defend the entrance to Puget Sound.

It is easy to explore but a flashlight would be very helpful inside the windowless rooms. Four six inch guns were installed here.

No ghosts or haunting's appeared to us in the daylight, but I'm not anchoring anywhere near here after dark. Day use only for me.

Victoria

Canada

- Dock   Yes
- Campsites   No
- Water   Yes
- Anch. Buoys   No
- Shopping   Yes
- Bathroom   Yes
- Fee   Yes
- Fire rings   No
- Dinghy Beach   No

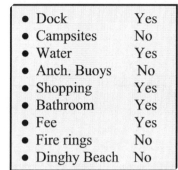

Cruise Rating
1 to 10

0 1 2 3 4 5 6 7 8 9 10

■ Anchoring 0   ■ 8

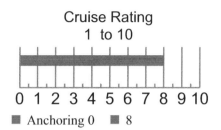

Going by boat to be a tourist in Victoria is an excellent idea and here are some reasons why. Most people go by car and a car is useless or worse, its in the way. Everything is an easy walk from the inner harbor where you will berth directly in front of the Empress Hotel.

No visit would be complete without a trip to Butchart Gardens and they have double decker shuttle buses running back and forth all day until closing, even late shuttle buses for the Saturday night fireworks.

When you arrive in the inner harbor be sure to scoot over to one side or risk getting buzzed and then yelled at for blocking seaplane access. Go straight to the red customs dock over toward the left side,. Check in by phone on the dock, then go over to the docks right in front of the concrete seawall, in front of the Empress. Grab an empty space and make your self at home. The bathrooms are to the left, the museum is to the right, mimes and street musicians are all around, and you catch the shuttle to Butchart in front of your boat. What could be easier?

Canada

• Dinghy Dock	Yes
• Campsites	No
• Water	No
• Anch. Buoys	Yes
• Hiking	Yes
• Bathroom	Yes
• Fee	No
• Fire rings	No
• Anchorage - - - Huge	

Cruise Rating
1 to 10

0 1 2 3 4 5 6 7 8 9 10

■ Anchoring 8   ■ Visiting 9

Butchart Gardens, wow. Indescribable as a destination. You need to come here if you like flowers. There are five free buoys talking distance from the dinghy dock where you will pay to get in. If you can't get a buoy just motor around the corner and anchor anywhere you want in a long still inlet (Tod) and paddle back to the dinghy dock. We like to walk the gardens late in the afternoon, then wait for the sun to set and walk again under the lights. I recommend you do the same. Then head for the boat for dinner and bed on the smoothest calmest inlet you have ever seen. Tip: on Saturday nights all summer they shoot off fireworks, no extra charge.

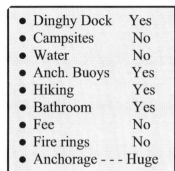

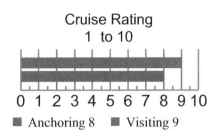

Canada

- Dock — Yes
- Campsites — Yes
- Water — Yes
- Anch. Buoys — Yes
- Hiking — Yes
- Bathroom — Yes
- Fee — Yes
- Fire rings — Yes
- Dinghy Beach — Yes

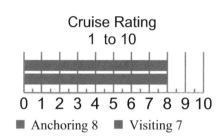

Cruise Rating
1 to 10

0 1 2 3 4 5 6 7 8 9 10

■ Anchoring 8   ■ Visiting 7

Sidney Spit Park is a favorite park for residents of Sidney out for a day or an overnighter, so don't be surprised to meet a lot of Canadians in their own park. This is a nice park with established shelters and hiking trails. The rangers live on the island so things are kept up. Out on the water are long docks and lots of buoys.

We have found Sidney Spit useful as a place to wait out bad weather or foggy conditions on Haro Strait before coming back to the US. Don't forget you can't stop here until you go to Sidney and check in, which is why we stop on the way back.

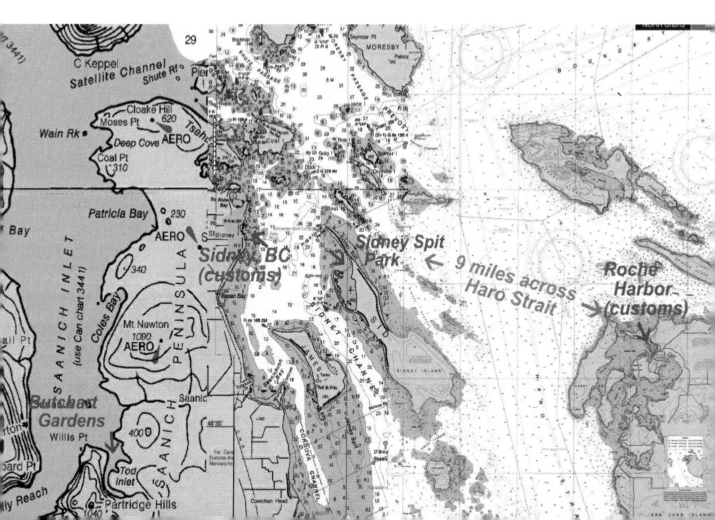

1

Dealing with Customs

If you plan to leave the area and run across to Canada there will be a few things to consider. First off, do not use this guide or any other as your last up to date source of information. Over the years our border crossing procedures have changed. Interestingly, reports of difficulty at vehicle points of entry seem to be much more prevalent than our cruiser points of entry. Perhaps cruisers are more likable. Do yourself a favor and check for new rules before you go. A simple web search and phone call may be all that's needed. Below is the web site where information and phone numbers are found for Customs and Border Protection.

www.cbp.gov/xp/cgov/travel/pleasure_boats/boats/pleasure_boat_overview.xml

Our last crossing in 2013 was as sweet as can be, and here is what I think is current information. You may drive your boat through Canadian waters and around their islands all you want, but you can't touch land until you check in. Before you may go ashore, you must check in. For our purposes the check in places are at Victoria or Sidney. Upon arrival (24/7) at the customs dock you will find a phone on a pole and nothing else. There is no office, just a phone. Have a piece of paper and a pencil handy, then just pick up the receiver and say hello. A friendly voice will want to know your names, ages, and boat type, name, age and number. They may ask where you're going and for how long. That's it, they will give you a number, write it down and tape it to your window so its visible from the dock where ever you tie up. Now that your checked in you may go anywhere you want and touch things, just remember to plan your visit around checking in before you go anywhere else. When you leave Canada, just go. There is no checking out required for either country.

Coming back to the states is a little more serious. Just like Canada you may not touch anything until you check in. This makes trip planning more difficult because running to Roche or Bellingham may be out of your way. You are not allowed to spend the night at Stuart or Sucia and then check in the next morning, you must check in first, then back track to where you really want to go. At Roche Harbor simply tie up at the red painted customs dock out on the end, you can't miss it. Everyone must stay on the boat, they are not allowed to run up the float to use the bathroom until later. One person from your boat must walk into the office on the float and present your passports and identification for everyone on board.

They will ask similar questions to what the Canadians asked and they will want that Canadian number, so don't lose it. Fresh fruits seems to be an issue so we try not to bring any back. Canned and sealed food stuffs are no problem. We have never had our boats searched or any

Customs phone at the Port of Sidney

issues except once when I made a joke that failed to bring a smile or even a hint of friendliness. Children need identification, but not passports. (this may change or have an age requirement, and is something I would find out beforehand) Adults need passports, and you can apply for them at your post office. Plan ahead, passports may take several months to arrive.

If it is a busy sunny weekend there will be other boats circling and waiting for your space at the customs dock so you must move along and find another place to dawdle or dally about. Only then may your crew go to the restroom.

Launching Ramps

Squalicum Harbor in Bellingham is by far the best ramp and facility around, and has my highest recommendation. If your planning to go to Sucia for the first night, Squalicum Harbor is the closest.

Squalicum Harbor Tip: this is where you want to go.
- Four lanes, suitable at all tide levels, open 24/7
- Lots of free parking, long or short term (this is a $100+ savings)
- Fresh water wash down hoses (always wash your trailer immediately after immersion, don't wait until you return a week later.)
- On site restaurants, and bathrooms with showers.
- Transient boat docks for overnight visits
- Major stores near by, but not walking distance
- Closest jump off point to Sucia, Matia and Patos Islands
- Fuel dock, pump out

Next on the list of popular launching points is

Cap Sante in Anacortes

- Two sling launches (big and little) but no ramp (keeping your trailer out of salt water is a good thing) may require reservation or waiting in line, not 24/7 use
- Fee parking, long term, short term (rv parking too) fees add up fast
- Restaurants, bathrooms, showers
- Transient boat docks for overnight visits
- A few major stores near by (short walk)
- Fuel dock, pump out
- Closest to Friday Harbor and inner island area

Launching Ramps

Not very far, but overlooked is

La Conner on the Swinomish Channel

- Big and little travel lifts (sling) at several marinas (will need reservations)
- One lane ramp with float, 24/7 use, all tides except minus
- Inexpensive, limited parking at ramp but lots of pay parking at marinas
- Transient docks for overnights at marina and along city seawall (really nice stopover place for lunch or the night at three city floats)
- Restaurants, quite a few, all walking distance
- No major stores but a very well stocked local store is a short walk
- Fuel and pump outs
- Closest to Deception Pass and heading south to Puget Sound area

Best kept secret is

Cornet Bay at Deception Pass State Park

Cornet Bay is my second ramp choice, and I use it if my plans call for easy access to the southern area, and most importantly long term hassle free parking and 24/7 usage. (daily fee) Excellent choice for car camping with boat.

- Four lane all tides ramps and floats
- Lots of long term fee parking ($10+ day)
- Transient floats for overnights
- Small convenience store, short walk
- Hiking trails
- Small bathroom
- You have the option of going through nearby Deception Pass or using Swinomish channel to avoid weather issues.
- On shore campgrounds

Launching Ramps

Washington Park in Anacortes

City park (campground) with ramp. This is your #1 choice for car camping with a boat. You can go out for day trips, and then keep the boat on the trailer at your camp site. Or splash the boat and take off for a week or more. Parking fee used to be $8 day. Calling for reservations is a must for camping.

- Two lane ramp, and float (sometimes part covered with sand and seaweed)
- Limited amount of fee parking, but long term is ok, or park at your camp site
- Subject to wakes
- Bathrooms (nice kybo's)
- No overnight boat tie up, but you could anchor out
- On shore campground, would make good home base for day only boating or large groups where some stay in camp while others go boating.
- Just a few miles to stores in town
- Absolute closest jump off point to San Juans

Twin Bridges

County ramp at north end of Swinomish Channel, under the bridge.(I have used once, I didn't like it)

- Two lane ramp with float
- Strong current a lot of the time
- Shallow at low tide (too shallow to use for most boats at low tide)
- Horrible stinky bathroom
- Questionable security in long term fee parking lot
- No stores, no nothing

Oak Harbor

Oak Harbor is best used as a fuel stop when heading north or south because its a little ways too far south, but it is a viable option for you.

- Ramp and travel lift
- Long term parking
- Stores are a few mile drive
- Really not needed, others are much closer
- Fuel and pump out

Fuel and Sustenance Stops

Fuel is readily available, (gas or diesel) and at mostly reasonable prices. You should not expect late hours or expect boat services at fuel docks. Remember 1/3 out 1/3 to get back and 1/3 for reserve just in case.
Tip *We fill our tanks when we can, not when we need it.*

1. **Anacortes:** (Cap Sante)

2. **La Conner** on Swinomish Channel
3. **Cornet Bay** Marina at Deception Pass
4. **Squalicum Harbor** in Bellingham
5. **Blakelys** at Peavine Pass on Blakely Island

6. **West beach resort** on north side of Orcas
7. **Fisherman Bay** on Lopez Island
8. **Friday Harbor:** San Juan Island
9. **Roche Harbor:** San Juan Island
10. **Deer Harbor** Orcas Island
11. **Rosario Resort** Orcas Island

Anacortes (Cap Sante)
Fuel dock is in front of main office and Safeway is across the street, but you will be asked to move away from fuel dock after fueling while you run for provisions.
(360) 293-0694. For fuel and slip assignments or (Harbor Master) VHF #66

La Conner on Swinomish Channel:
The fuel dock is at the north end of town and they have a very small selection in the store, but if you move south after fueling about a 1/4 mile and tie up at one of the three public floats you can walk one block to the main store in La Conner (Pioneer market) where they have everything you could want, including ice and wine. The floats at the seawall are self serve with a pay kiosk at the top of the gangplanks. Public bathrooms are very close on the main street. (We like La Conner a lot)
Harbor Master and office at marina 360-466-3118   VHF #66

Cornet Bay Marina at Deception Pass:
For groceries only, tie up at the State Park floats and walk 1/4 mile to a small convenience store or take boat right to fuel dock at next facility over and save the walk. (360) 675-5411

Squalicum Harbor in Bellingham:
Fuel dock, but groceries are a healthy walk. We have been told, they run a shuttle during the day time, but we always have our car. Bellingham is a major city and has anything you need. Harbor Master – VHF # 16 or (360) 676-2542

Blakelys at Peavine Pass on Blake Island: 360 375-6121
Easy and convenient fuel and small grocery store with deli counter.   Plenty of room at the float and no rush, we sit on the lawn and eat ice cream each time we stop by..
General store and Marina Harbor Master, (360) 375-6121

West beach resort on north side of Orcas near Sucia:
Easy and handy if your at Sucia or taking the northern route.
Fuel dock and general grocery store with deli.
(watch your draft at low tide) (360) 375-6121   or   (877)937-8224

Fisherman Bay on Lopez Island:
Islander Resort and Marina, fuel and store - Harbor Master (360) 468-2233
Watch your draft at entrance to bay at low tide
(check the article about dinghy access to Lopez village under Lopez Island group)

Friday Harbor: San Juan Island:
Fuel dock, short walk to large grocery store on main street
360-378-2688 or call Harbor Master on #66 for slips

Roche Harbor: San Juan Island:
Fuel dock, well stocked grocery store right at top of gang plank, restaurants
Slip assignment 800.586.3590 or Harbor Master vhf #78

Deer Harbor Orcas Island
Fuel dock, small store and deli out on dock
(360) 376-3037

Rosario Resort Orcas Island:
Fuel dock, store and restaurant just a short walk, you can leave boat at float while you shop and eat.
    (360) 376-2222   Harbor Master vhf #78 or 360-376-2152

    Each of the fuel stops listed have *transient docks available for overnight stays,* but there is no guarantee they will have room so you should call ahead once you know for sure where your headed.

Some tips about fuel

Seems like I missed a gas station somewhere, Oak Harbor, Port Townsend, hmmm! No, that's all there is.

Did you know most marinas (probably a law) forbid you to fill your tank from a portable container while in your slip or on the property? (You may spill some in the water or start a raging inferno)

Tip Just a thought for you to remember; Several times at fuel stops I have been told by the operator that they will wait a little after closing if I call and tell them I'm on my way. The numbers listed, will go to the office or harbor master. You will need to ask for the fuel dock or number.

Tip You need to manage your fuel consumption and what you carry. If you are new to boating you may mistakenly treat your boat like you do your car. (I'll have a bucks worth of premium please) You can't walk to the gas station or call for a delivery without a huge expense, and running out somewhere may be life threatening. Deciding to cross a strait or motor a long distance with barely enough fuel is a beginners mistake.

When the wind (waves) or current catches you by surprise, your planned fuel consumption goes out the window, your two gallon per hour rate goes to ten or more gallons, and your planned one hour crossing becomes five, or worse, and then you end up not where you planned.

It is quite acceptable to carry extra portable tanks on deck, just remember to secure them, keep fumes out of the bilge, and have a way to safely transfer fuel to your operating tank.

Tip I can't stress enough the importance of the last tip .

Tip: *"Never approach a float faster than you are willing to hit it"*

92

- Water temp --The water is too cold to swim, but kids sometimes jump in anyway.
- PWC -- Jet Skis are outlawed in San Juan county.
- Wind -- Not much wind. The San Juans are not known for great sailing winds in July and August. Out in the straits (Haro, Rosario, Georgia, Juan De Fuca) you may get some decent sailing, but inside the islands it will be spotty if at all.
- Bathrooms -- All the parks have nice composting toilets, (each island mentioned for overnight is a park) the rangers service all parks on a regular basis. You will be pleasantly surprised at how clean the facilities are. Drinking water is available at only a few parks, bring your own!
- Pets -- Pets (dogs) must be on leash all the time, everywhere.
- Garbage service -- your kidding right? pack it in, pack it out. Most resorts/marinas have dumpsters, but zero at parks. Tip: repackage and leave the bulk at home.
- Mooring fees -- .60 cents a foot at park floats, $10-12? for buoys, $.75- $1.75 per foot at resort slips.
- Emergency's -- Yes, call 911, call the Coast Guard on channel 16, call vessel assist services. Cell phone service is very good in most areas, but not at Rosario for some reason.
- Dumping -- Nothing over the side, period, and you are not allowed to empty holding tanks into the water anywhere. Pump out stations are located at most resorts, ports and marinas, but not at any parks.
- Crowds -- Yes, No, ? It is very unlikely that anywhere you arrive will not be able to accommodate your boat because you will always be prepared to anchor and use your dinghy.
- Reservations -- If your cruise plan is to only go to resorts and you have no dinghy or intention to anchor out, then you should secure reservations before you go. If you are flexible and able to bend a little then just go and let your cruise evolve before you.
- Insects-mosquitoes, never seen any, don't tell anyone. But some of the little bird reserve islands have flies a half mile offshore, you've been warned.
- Temperature -- Pretty moderate days and nights in the summer, but if you don't bring sunblock and warm foul weather gear, whose to blame.
- Orcas -- You will have to go look for whales out in the straits, they don't come into the inner island areas. You may get lucky and see them when your in their areas off of Lime Kiln but probably not, sorry. Seals Porpoise, Dolphins, Eagles, Deer, Raccoon's, Otters are everywhere you go.
- Fires on shore -- yes, except on Matia Island.

Ten Things to Know

1. Expenses:

DNR buoys are free (Cypress Island) State Park buoys are $10-$12 many park floats are .60 cents a foot, Marinas charge between 75 cents and $2 a foot. Gasoline is a little more expensive than on land, but not much more. Food, groceries, ice are just a little more than the mainland but very fair priced overall.

2. How many days to plan:

You could do a weekend outing if you are in the area already, but I recommend a minimum of four days, or up to two weeks depending on what you like to do. (I like to sit on the dock at Jones Island and read my book between naps and walks, then I make a campfire in an empty tent site and cook Kielbasa on a stick, followed by a glass of wine. Then retire to my boat for a good nights sleep. The next day, I do it again, the days just zoom by)
Tip: don't try to see and do everything, instead plan another trip just as soon as you can, and another, and another.

3. Salt Water:

Salt water dry's sticky and does not suds up well with soap, you will get it all over you and your boat, count on it. After a week you will look forward to a shower. Your boat will be covered with salt crystals. Marinas in the islands have little water and don't want you washing your boat. Squalicum Harbor in Bellingham has boat and trailer fresh water wash down hoses in the parking lot. You should use them each time you dunk your trailer.

4. Provisions:

For the most part you will want to provision before you leave on the boat. Anacortes and Bellingham have all the big stores and each has a West Marine store. All the resorts and towns have grocery stores, if you drive a fast boat, supply's may be only minutes away, putt putt's should work a store visit into your circuit. I say circuit because most cruisers will follow a circle of some sort trying to hit many stops. We find that ice needs renewing after three days, so a stop over at Friday Harbor, Deer Harbor, Roche Harbor, Blakelys, or Orcas landing fits the bill. All these places have fuel and showers. Showers will cost a handful of quarters so be quick about it, or be poor. Cold showers brrr are free at many places.

5. Garbage:

All the parks are pack it in and pack it out, the marinas have dumpster's. If you are new to boat camping you will find garbage to be a pain because you are not used to storing everything in your boat. Little things like empty water bottles suddenly take space you don't have. You must give careful thought to what your bringing, and the garbage it will generate. We don't use disposable bottles, minimize pop consumption, and try to have campfires to burn burnable trash (not plastic). It is against the law to toss anything, (even an apple core) in the water.

6. Animals: (pets)

Your dogs must be on a leash, period, everywhere. Raccoon's are on all islands and will climb right into your boat or kayak in the day time if you let them. Deer are all over too, but they shy away, except on Jones Island where some are mooches. Otters live under most floats and docks, they will crawl all over your boat, get into things and make a mess. Otters also will mark their territory by pooing on your stuff, dock lines are a favorite. I try to remind myself that the animals are full time residents, and we are simply visitors.

7. Bathrooms:

All the parks have nice composting toilets, (each island mentioned for overnight is a park) the rangers service all parks on a regular basis. You will be pleasantly surprised at how clean the facilities are.

8. Where to go:

Your destination is simply that, its the journey getting there and the experiences on the way that make a trip a wonderful vacation. Try the contents for the list of destination parks and descriptions. Tip Its very easy to go with no plan at all, just let your trip develop one day at a time.

9. Launching ramps:

Hands down first choice is Squalicum Harbor in Bellingham, next consider Deception Pass at Cornet Bay, then Washington Park in Anacortes or the La Conner city ramp, last choice go to Twin Bridges, under the bridges on the way to Anacortes.

These are all public ramps, there are many yards with travel lifts and light duty sling systems. There are ramps throughout the San Juans but that would require a ferry ride and so are not listed.

10. Emergency's:

Here are some ideas. Bring your cell phone and boat charger, have a hard copy list of numbers to call. Tip don't depend on a saved list on your phone or laptop. Try to bring a portable handheld marine radio, bring basic first aid kit, for help call 911. You can call the Coast Guard or Sheriff on the phone or radio, they can be there pretty fast, or arrange for vessel assist on your credit card. If you are worried or extra needy you could take two boats, and go cruising with good friends. Don't forget, the boating community is a great resource whether you need an aspirin, nuts and bolts, or help retrieving your dinghy.

Planning your Cruise

T his is a really subjective task, which means you need to take charge and figure out your first trip, but I'll try to get you going.

1st It would really help your planning if you go back and review some of what I hope you have read already. Re-read the resource section *Q & A's plus Ten things you need to know.*

2nd keep in mind your goals. Fishing?, Hiking? Sailing? Camping? Obviously a family with young kids will have much different ideas of what constitutes a fun time.

3rd Think about your boats ability's, I try to not talk sailing versus power versus a whole lot of power, but when I say boat ability, I mean motoring not sailing, you should not make plans where sailing to your destination is a requirement. Sailing should be considered a bonus when time allows that you may or may not be rewarded.

All planning to get from point A to point B should be around motoring distances and times, not sailing.

So, if you will be cruising with a putt putt at 4-6 mph, you should not plan to crisscross the San Juans on twenty five mile runs unless you set aside most of a day. Don't forget your speed over ground with an adverse current may be down to 2-3 mph. On the other hand, fast planing boat skippers will discover their destination may be just an easy two hour sprint.

4th Decide your time frame. I know many people have a week or ten days for vacation and that's that. Because weather plays such a big role in your plan you should be flexible. I suggest you not get

> *Now that I have made an anti-sailing warning, you need to know that some of our best cruises have been where I refused to use the auxiliary. One trip we sailed from Friday Harbor right to*  *the dock at Jones, then the next day we sailed off the float at Jones and made it around Orcas to our anchorage at Lummi, all under sail. Personal achievements or goals are just as valid as making a destination.(even if two days later) We used the currents and sailed, but threw the clock and destinations out the window. My only plan that trip was to use as little fuel as possible and go sailing as much as possible. We ended up going 120 miles and used under five gallons in a week. (Much further if you count the many tacks)*

pinned down to a tight schedule. We try to allow one or more extra days that are unscheduled, for example we might plan a five day trip to Matia, Roche, Jones, and Pelican Beach, but allow time away from home and work to take a seven day trip. This way if we want, we can stay at Jones (I wish) an extra night, plus divert through Deception Pass, skip Roche for Friday Harbor and run down to Cattle Pass to watch whales off of Lime Kiln.

I know that example seemed like I had no plan at all but that is exactly how we have one great cruise after another.   Our last planned visit to Butchart Garden involved just a goal. *Get to Butchart Garden and bicycle some along the way.* The cruise ended up being six nights, and I will outline briefly below how it developed. But first #5 (the most important)

5th *Set a date and start packing.* For your first cruise plan I suggest that you adopt some of our loose attitude, add your own needs and desires, and forge ahead.

Read our six day wander to
Butchart Garden

We departed our slip in La Conner in mid morning after a relaxing breakfast and headed for Cypress Island. Anchored at Pelican Beach and hiked to the top of Eagle Bluff. Up anchor, cross Rosario, slip through Obstruction Pass and arrive for night at Olga float. 2nd day, did some reading and dinghy sailing, departed after lunch for float at Eastsound and bicycled town, moved over and anchored in Judd Bay at nightfall. 3rd morning, swung over to Rosario, tied up for free next to gas dock and took three and half hour ride up, up, up to Morrow State Park and Lake Constitution, almost burn up brakes coming back. Cast off and leisurely motored all the way to Jones Island. Anchored (to save fee) in plenty of time for sundown'ish west loop hike and evening campfire on shore.

4th morning, listened to weather forecast, checked tides, then timed mid morning departure to cross Haro Strait during slack water, after quick customs check in at Sidney arrived at Tod inlet and rowed dingy to Butchart in time for afternoon walk around,

"Not all who cruise are lost"

and then repeated with after dark walk around. Spent hour or so as darkness fell listening to concert on lawn and then paddled in dark back to boat, had great evening at anchor. 5th morning, upped anchor really early at 6am, made coffee underway to beat forecast storm out on Haro Strait, checked in with customs at Roche around noon, attempted bike ride and got derailed due to county workers paving and oiling road. Left Roche, drove right past Friday and anchored fifty feet from Odlin Park float. Used two anchors that night trying to keep bow into waves with not much success. Up several times during night, dragged one anchor. 6th morning, wonderful morning considering the floppy night., after long breakfast, biked most of Lopez until exhausted, moved over to James in time for anchoring but nabbed space at the dock.

7th morning, hiked perimeter trail and over summit, read some, wrote some, dinghy sailed some, watched eagles, sat around James all day, departed with just enough time to cross Rosario and get back to La Conner by dark.

I think that was a six day trip, and we can't wait to do it again, except we will substitute Victoria for two days, skip Butchart, and Lopez, and add docking at Friday Harbor for biking San Juan Island again.

There you have it, a very workable low key plan to go to Butchart Garden, with an Victoria option. You can tell by our wanderings before and after the Butchart visit that we were entirely flexible and just let things develop, in fact we had wanted to spend time shopping at Sidney but the port wanted $15 per hour to use a slip, so I said forget you and moved on. BTW they wanted $5/hr to tie our dinghy to the dinghy dock if we anchored out. What's with that anti cruiser policy?

Throughout this guidebook are many tips and suggestions, if you heed them you will probably have a great time. For instance, somewhere is a tip about not navigating in the dark. If you ignore that warning and try to cross an ocean of frothy water as the sun sets so you can meet your self imposed schedule, you can expect to have a story to tell afterwards. I know, I been there, done that. I read a comment once somewhere about this skipper that never had any issues. All his trips were boring, he seemed to be blessed with good gear, good crew, good luck, and good weather all the time. I wonder what his secret was, do you suppose he just took his time. Tip, Learn where the out of the way anchorages are hiding and don't hesitate to call it a day before you're in trouble, then you will be a little like that boring skipper.

An idea for your first trip

Go the first night or two or three to a camping type place. Next, go to Friday Harbor and anchor out or get a slip, and eat in town. (Get showers, buy ice, get fuel) Walk all around and visit the whale museum. Next go to another boat camping, place. Repeat at Roche Harbor.

If you're more of a resort type, try this. First night(s) go to Friday Harbor, then Roche Harbor, then Fisherman Bay, now Rosario, your good to go.

We met a couple cruising in a dory style camper yacht, when I asked where they were staying they said they have a slip at Friday Harbor for seven days that they return to each night. Their car and trailer was parked at Squalicum Harbor. *Pretty darn good plan!*

Get a Chart

At some point you need to get a paper chart. I can hear some of you already saying, *but I have a 3D GPS chart plotter with every chart in the whole world built right in.* By all means use it everywhere you go. But your car has good tires right? And yet you also carry a spare tire. End of discussion. Tip Get NOAA #18421 Strait of Juan De Fuca to Strait of Georgia. It covers Bellingham Bay to Deception Pass and Swinomish Channel all the way over to the edge of Vancouver Island with Victoria and then up to some of the Canadian Gulf Islands. Disappointingly, it does not show Butchart Gardens but you will get by just fine.

There is a larger scale chart available, but I won't get into or argue scale size. This is the one I have and I'm happy with it. Tip Protect your chart, or there will come a day when it needs to be replaced, and then you will wish you had taken better care of it. I sandwich mine between two sheets of Acrylic held together with contact cemented velcro strips. In an open windy cockpit or rainy day my homemade chart protector is a god send.

On the chart/map subject, I also have a bunch of plastic coated maps from fishnmap.com These maps cover large areas and are very useful, they are under $10 including postage. We have a few colorful semi topo maps that are really easy to look at for planning discussions. Over the years we have enjoyed drawing a different colored line for each cruise and then dating the line for future reference and nostalgia. But we ran out of colors and the map became so covered with crisscrossing lines, many going to the same hot spots time and again that we quit writing on it a long time ago. We still carry the maps and miscellaneous guidebooks with us in a zippered lap top bag.

GPS and Depth Sounder

You don't need either one but I would try my darnndest to have both on board, even if only handheld. Tip:There are just too many ways they will save your bacon. Or for those unfamiliar with the bacon term, think *keep you off the rocks.* Even in perfect clear weather if you're unfamiliar with the landscape, from four or five miles out you will not be able to dead reckon. You will have to study your chart, take compass bearings and do it all the old fashioned way. Don't get me wrong, chart navigation is great fun in the straits and islands but do it by choice not because you have to. In fog or overcast conditions, a GPS is like having a personal pilot on board, only this one never gets lost. We use a 15.6" lap top with a chart plotter program and a USB antenna. The store bought package came with every NOAA chart installed, I love it, the big screen is so much bigger than all my obsolete chart plotters, and the whole shebang cost just $100 plus the lap top. No it's not 3D, but at $100, I'm very happy.

For a depth sounder we use a $79 Humminbird fish finder. Same story, these two tools make all the difference, allowing us to have perfect cruises spending our time on what we enjoy.

An old salt once said, I only worry around land, that is where the shallow water is. Well the San Juan's have got lots of land and most of it is ringed with shallow water but you don't need to worry. For the most part, there are not a bunch of reefs or coral heads sticking up in the middle of nowhere. The occasional rock or two or three (ok, hundreds) are marked and charted. This does not mean you can put her on auto and go below, you will still have to keep watch. Flotsam and anchored crab fishing floats are likely to be anywhere, even where you may think it's a main channel. This is an active logging area so logs will occasionally need to be dodged and some will become nasty deadheads. The worlds cruising grounds are full of accidents, million dollar losses, and narrow escapes because inattentive skippers thought they could get away with sloppy boating habits. When conditions on board prevent us from keeping good watch we simply slow her down, or stop, it's that simple.

When planning your cruise, you need to expect and prepare for big waves in the straits, cold winds, rain, and fog. Hold up a sec. hold on, its not that bad, I just want to prepare you for the worst, that way if things don't go exactly as planned you will be able to handle it and have a great cruise anyway.

First off, is Rosario Strait, like it or not, everyone must deal with a four mile crossing. The only way around Rosario is flying, or not to go cruising.

When the wind and tidal current are at odds, there will be several hours of sloppy conditions that your admiral or first mate may not enjoy. Your choices are, tuff it out and cross anyway, wait a while at some cool hide away, or perhaps modify your destination and course to make life on board better while crossing the strait. On our cruises, we have done all of the above at one time or another, and never let a little snotty weather ruin our day. (Ok, not ruin the entire day, err week) Most of the time if your course is uncomfortable you can change your heading for a smoother ride. Of course, that means changing your route and possibly traveling further and longer or to a different destination than intended.

Fog, fog, fog, god what horrible stuff. A lot of the time fog hangs around the straits. Sometimes for weeks at a time there will be fog outside Deception pass to Lopez or Thatcher Pass, but none at Peavine. There may be fog guarding Cattle Pass and off shore from Roche all the way across Haro Strait, but none in the inner island area or up at Sucia. You will simply have to go around it, go through it, or wait for it to clear.

If your coming up from the Seattle area and fog or big waters of Admiralty Inlet bothers you, stay on the Langley side of Whidbey Island, you will have less seas and can always duck through Swinomish Chanel if you hit fog at Deception Pass.

If you put in or start at Squalilcum Harbor or Cap Sante on the mainland, you have the choice of crossing Rosario at several places. Many times simply going around the other side of Cypress Island or Lummi Island makes a huge difference in waves and fog that you encounter.

Sooner or later you will need to cross Rosario from Guemes Channel to Thatcher Pass or some other pass and it will be pea soup fog. My recommendation is to not go unless you have a reliable GPS. The reason is simple, the current will drag you sideways and you will miss the pass, now what? Are you north or south of the pass? (A compass won't help) Don't forget, a GPS shows you where to go but it does not show you the ferry boat or show the ferry boat where you are. That takes radar, and buying radar just to cross a foggy strait is silly. Its better to be flexible and modify the big plan.

Let's talk a little more foggy, ok. Many times visibility is down to half a mile, so you scoot half a mile and then you can still see half a mile, but you can't see where your going or from whence you came. That's ok, with a half mile view you don't need to worry about running into anything, and most of the time all you will ever deal with is the four miles across Rosario.

Currents

If all your boating/sailing experience has been in lakes, you're in for a shock. The waters of the San Juan area move back and forth, and up and down constantly. At prominent headlands, it sometimes goes in circles, big circles. Along the edge of Rosario in Buroughs Bay it always flows North, and don't even try to figure out which way Swinomish Channel flows.

Skippers of sailboats and putt putts will suffer and connive ways to beat mother nature. Fast planning boats will be affected mostly in the pocketbook. There are NOAA sites throughout the area that tide level and tidal flow are forecast for, and you can see charts of the results all over the Internet. You can play around with the numbers and have a lot of fun making plans, but we find that even though we know when, where and how much to expect, we still go when we're ready and get to our destination sooner or later.

You should be realistic in your planning so you're not too surprised. I suggest that you simply add 1-3 mph to whatever your cruising speed is, if the current is with you. If the current is against you subtract 1-3 mph and leave it at that. As a general rule of thumb most of the waterways of the San Juans flow northward on a flood tide and southward on ebb. All the passes and headlands will have faster water at the narrowest points. There are some notable passes that will have high flows for an hour or so each way that may stop a slow boat dead in its own wake. Those putt putt skippers will want to time passage for slack high or slack low water. Deception Pass and the Narrows at Tacoma are two to be reckoned with. Dodd Narrows and Seymour Pass up north are favorites also.

Set and Drift

While we're talking currents, I am sure you know that your boat will be dragged sideways whilst you drive forward when crossing a channel. It is very easy to not pay enough attention to the currents "set and drift" and what's on the side of your boat. Let's put it simpler, if you're driving forward and looking forward you will miss what you're heading for sideways. It is easy when close to rocks to allow yourself to be dragged into them *because your looking where you want to go, not where you are really going.* Tip Please re-read that last sentence and load it into your default system, it may save your boat or someone important to you.

Thirty minutes after we anchored, the two rafted boats left so we had half the float at James to ourselves for the evening.

Ⅰf you are new to the San Juan's as well as not too experienced in cruising (boat camping) you may find some useful advice here. But some people just don't like being told what to bring or what not to bring, or ask for directions when they are hopelessly lost. So stop right here if you recognize yourself, you are probably like me and need to suffer some along the way.

OK now that the captain and skipper and male teenagers have quit reading lets see if we can ease the pain somewhat. Were not going to even try to be all inclusive here, but just some little reminders to get you thinking about your cruise. Obviously you have a spotless well equipped boat and many things are already on board.

Please, please, please, this is just a bunch of suggestions, you don't really need all this stuff to go for a boat ride. Some of the best trips (and worst) are minimalist, you know "kiss" (keep it simple stupid)

Here goes,

- I'll bet you don't have an underwater flashlight, they are great for attracting (teasing) sea creatures after dark, and will add hours of entertainment time to answer your children's "I'm bored" comments. (hint, stick a cheap led flashlight in a ziplock bag) Now tie it to the end of your boat hook and poke it under water.

- How about heavy duty zip lock bags, or the ones they sell at the outdoor outfitter stores for river running, you know for your cell phone, ipod, camera, wallet, etc, etc, etc.....

- Speaking of waterproof have you got any good wood matches in a waterproof container?

- Matches mean campfires, that means you need a folding pruning saw. (get a good nasty sharp one) Tip Leave the ax, machetes, and hatchets at home because, #1 they don't work well for gathering firewood, #2 someone may get hurt and your a long way from an ER. All we use is a nasty sharp little folding saw!

- Here's one you really miss and then its too late - chap-stick with spf 99 (how high do the #'s go?)

- Remember that hat that blew off into the water? ditto for glasses! you need a chin strap or leash.

- OK, this is good one, get a second or third corkscrew, uh huh! (try em at home first to make sure you can trust-em at dinner time)

- Dramamine in all forms for everyone.

- Cheap little led flashlights, lots of em, they're cheap.

- Plastic kites (not paper) for beach fun, don't forget the string.

- Multi-function tool that you carry in your pocket all the time.

- Boat cleaning supplies, wax, polish, paint thinner to remove tars you track on board with your shoes. We seem to do our heavy cleaning while on a cruise, I see others doing the same. Misc. boat repair supplies and tools. (sail tape, soft scrub)

Cruising is not a hole
in the water
I toss money into!

Tip Copy this list and add to it while making plans.
Keep a copy on your computer and update it as needed:

This list is intended for travel in general not just boating,
but you can figure what you -- oh just read it.

Much, much more to come, keep reading. Those were just some starter ideas for boaters. Since some folks really benefit by having in depth detailed instructions and are lost without to-do lists. They will find a list for general travel just for them.

Keep going>>

Checklist and Things to do at home before you leave, and on the day you leave:

- create a trip planner/outline "This could be a to-do list") add to it and edit often
- pay the bills
- turn off water heater
- turn down/off furnace
- cancel paper and stop routine deliveries (have the mail held at post office)
- tell the neighbor so they can watch your house for problems
- leave a list (itinerary) and keys (with friend, relative) where you are going
- leave extra keys with someone (you may need them mailed to you)
- emergency numbers (bring list, include all numbers, e-mails too)
- mow the lawn, arrange for sprinkler system operation or shut it down preferred
- arrange for pet and plant care
- make the house look lived in
- lock windows, doors, garage
- set the alarm
- set voice message
- forward calls
- turn off water
- deal with garbage service
- enable, disable computers, electronics
- unplug TV's and anything that uses a remote control or standby power
- credit/debit card info and what to do if stolen
- if your bringing a lap top, what about photo software, updates, make sure wifi works, charger, 12v inverter?

Vehicle checks before you go

- Tip The number one most important vehicle check is to grease your trailer bearings or possibly abort you entire cruise somewhere on the highway.
- Oil check, carry spare oil
- Tire pressure/condition (buy new tires for peace of mind)
- Spare tire and Jack (Jack will do the work)
- Check brake lining, master cylinder fluid
- Check hoses and carry spare coolant, atf.
- Check the belts, bring extra serpentine belt if you're traveling to or from a remote area.
- Tune up and service
- Wipers and washer fluid

- Battery check & connections, jumper cables
- Cell phone travel charger
- Do you know where and how to check fuses? (spares)
- Do you have a fire extinguisher? (Car and boat)

Shall we dispense with all the formal bullets, they just take up a lot of space., And we have a lot more to cover >>> next page please

More treasures to consider

First aid kit, plus prescriptions, etc: antibiotic/alcohol wipes (sealed), antiseptic cream, aspirin, motion sickness pills, bandages, burn ointment, elastic wrap, eye wash, hydrogen peroxide, Ibuprofen, insect repellent, sterile tape, scissors, snake bite kit, sterile gauze and pads, sun screen lotion, tweezers, Benadryl

Clothing:

Regular day wear, out on the town wear, shirts, t-shirts, trousers, jeans, dresses, sweater, raincoat, wind breaker, pajamas, swim wear, shorts, socks, joggers, hikers, sandals

Toiletries:

Brush, comb, toothbrush, toothpaste, floss, TP, soaps, shaving, sunscreen, deodorant, mirror, foot powder, scissors,

Children's clothing, toiletries: (who invited them anyway?)

Pets, needs, etc. (did you forget?) BTW dogs and cats are welcome, and many enjoy cruising, but we know of some dogs that get seasick. There are no parks where leash laws don't apply. Be sure to bring appropriate pfd's for pets.

**More items to help jog the old bean, plus some good things
to bring along but often forgot.**

Aluminum foil, camp cook kit, cooking oil, corkscrew, cutting board, flatware, spices, knife, measure cup, paper towels, plastic cups, trash bags, pot holder, tongs, spatula, matches, zip lock bags, flashlight, batteries, travel alarm, cell phone, gps, map, rain poncho, chocolate, pet needs! CASH, camera and tripod, medicines, hard copy of friends and relatives phone numbers in case your cell phone quits. weather report, books, sunglasses, binoculars, contact lens prep. hats, laundry/wash bags, mini sewing kit, playing cards and games, car inverter to run chargers >> this list is not all inclusive and needs your additions/subtractions as you prepare for your travels. More yet >>

Important numbers & things

Passwords for getting online and atm banking etc.

do not rely on cell phone or laptop memory for numbers/names/addresses (make a hard copy)

auto insurance info.   Your automobile license number (in case its stolen)

do you have current hard pictures of everyone?

serious medical condition information

106   passports, photo ID, vaccination proof, reservations, birth certificates

Had enough of lists ?

Don't toss in the towel just yet, but it is time to lighten up. This preparation exercise is really a one time thing that never gets completely finished. As you cruise again and again, you will simply add to your arsenal. Usually when you realize you forgot something like marshmallow & hot dog sticks., You improvise. Aha, now use your pocket multi tool and cut some sticks (crisis averted).

Remember that minimalist comment at the beginning of this chapter, it may have some merit. *Kiss*

Tip: One of the first things to learn about packing is that you can't bring everything, and that everything you bring must fit in the boat. The problem with packing the boat is that you when you start unpacking and using stuff, everything expands, then it won't fit in the boat and you are forced to wallow in the mess.

There are no trash cans at any parks!!

It pays to consolidate at home, avoid unnecessary packaging, plan meals and snacks that don't generate trash. Avoid bringing cases and cases of drinks and other plastics. Have a plan for containing trash and on longer outings arrange to visit marinas.

The dinghy may be used as a trash can, which works well but attracts birds, raccoons and otters. Otters can swim you know, and they hang out under the floats.

Tip: When asleep, keep everything on deck tightly sealed or suffer!!

"Cruising may not be exciting all the time, But it's certainly not boring all the time"

Bicycling and Boating in the San Juan's

"Let's go bicycling while on our cruise." It's not as crazy as it first sounds. After staring at miles of water and seemingly endless tree lined monotonous shore, I'm ready to swim to the nearest island. Well not really, the waters too cold and who would anchor the boat.

You should answer a few basic questions first, before planning a bike hike.

- Can you carry bikes on the boat or car while traveling down the highway?
- Can you carry one or more bikes on your boat?

One time we carried three bicycles on our sailboat and every time we tacked, we snagged the jib sheets. The bikes blocked going forward on one side. One bike in the dinghy with me padding was a comedy, two bikes, a farce, and three was an accident waiting to happen. Will I do it again? You bet I will.

Tip we learned to tie the bikes outside the shrouds and lifelines keeping the decks clear, it worked well.

- Is it ok for them to get salty?
- Some Islands have no roads and bikes on trails are forbidden so plan accordingly.

Ok, now that the obvious questions are addressed, let's talk some realities so you will have more to think about while planning your next cruise.

- Lopez Island, Orcas, and San Juan are the only islands to consider biking, so your bicycles will be in the way when you are visiting Jones, James and Patos.

This boat is equipped for shore fun with a couple bikes aboard.

- A decent bike ride will probably eat up the whole day, so you may want to stay put for a couple days and not weigh anchor late in the day after a long ride.

- Is everyone participating, how will you handle non-riders?

- Flat tires and emergency's, things don't break until you are ten miles away from home or the boat. Do you have the skills and tools to make likely repairs?

- There will be no bike lanes, can you handle carzy drivers?

*Bicycling and boating in the San Juan's,
are definitely compatible.*

We have rode (ridden?) our bicycles on all three Islands, some more, some less. For easy riding, level Lopez can't be beat. San Juan offers the most to see and do, but riding to the top of Mt Constitution on hilly Orcas Island is a real achievement and worthy goal.

Our worst bike ride started at Roche Harbor and wasn't bad at all, just disappointing because it was aborted almost before we started out. We were anchored quite a way from the dinghy dock so I put the outboard on the dinghy, two bikes in front of me hanging over both sides and off I went for dry land telling Linda I would be right back for her. Well, I was right back but bikes and my dinghy are not a match made in heaven, and getting them off the dinghy at the high dock at Roche proved tricky indeed.

Our planned ride to Lime Kiln was cut short when we headed out only to find road paving in progress before we even go off the property. Not wanting to bring any tar back to the boat we changed plans and were back on board in a couple hours. We weighed anchor and went to Odlin Park on Lopez Island, and the next day had a hugely enjoyable all day ride. Lime Kiln will have to wait for another time.

Our best ride started at Friday Harbor where we rented a slip for two nights. We started in the morning after a leisurely late breakfast by pushing our bikes up the ramp and then rode out to American Camp, then after a snack we headed over the hill to Lime Kiln, and finished up circling back by way of the Lavender Garden. Having the boat in a slip waiting for our return was comforting; I didn't worry about being late or on time, but a few creeps noticed our good looks and honked at us along the way.

So there you have it, having a float or dock greatly helps getting the bike off and on the boat, but a dinghy works too. I highly recommend planning a combined bike and boat trip, the variations on how, who, when and where are endless.

Tip: *Here is an idea for a combination event to get you thinking of the possibilities.*

We planned a trip one year where two of our daughters would not stay with us for the duration, instead they left early and rode the ferry From Friday back to Anacortes as foot passengers. They had previously left their car at the ferry terminal in long term parking. *Eastward ferry travel is free,* that's right you only pay to get out to the islands, the ride back is free. Our daughters could just as easily have taken bicycles, or they could have paid the minimal foot and bike fare and met us at Orcas Landing, or Lopez. I hope you see the possibilities for a group effort, even a reunion in the islands is easily accomplished and at little expense.

Bicycles, boats, ferries and free rides are at your disposal. **Be creative!**

Locations with docks for loading bicycles

San Juan Island
- Roche Harbor
- Garrison Bay
- Friday Harbor

Lopez Island
- Odlin County Park
- Islander Resort or Islands Marine Center (Fisherman Bay)

Orcas Island
- Olga
- Eastsound
- Rosario Resort
- Orcas Landing
- Deer Harbor Resort
- West Beach Resort

Most of the time you will be able to pull in and unload the bikes and then anchor nearby, but a dinghy option might solve any *"no vacancy's"* that are thrown at you. As for me, I unload the bikes while fueling, then go anchor and come back to the dinghy dock. Have fun!

Tip: Apply some sort of protective messy spray on your bicycle before you get it salty.

"Bicycles and inflatable's may not get along well together"

Inflatable's?

Hiking vs Strolling

Is strolling on your cruise agenda?

When does a casual stroll or walk become a hike? Let's see, if I gain two hundred feet in ten minutes, I'm going to notice it. If I walk for five miles and then five back, I will sleep very well that night.

Below is a list of the places I really enjoy strolling followed by a list of hiking ideas.

1. Saddlebag Island has a perimeter trail that takes less than hour and may be walked in sandals.

2. Doe Island takes ten minutes including a stop at the head. (Head means kybo in another language, many years ago we just said outhouse. The one on Doe is of the old fashioned variety)

3. Jones's Island trails and James's trails are very similar except Jones's trails don't have any cliffs you might fall off while day dreaming.

4. Matia Island's perimeter trail is our favorite stroll. It takes about an hour and is interspersed with short side jaunts to hidden miniature coves. The section across the middle is as close to a rain forest you will find in the San Juan's. Tip: Don't miss strolling Matia, even if you have to anchor in the cove at the other end of the island.

5. Stuart Island has two anchorages and they share a common narrow isthmus where you will access the islands primary trail out to the lighthouse. Whether you're at Prevost Harbor or Reid Harbor you will still start your walk/hike at the same place and be greeted by a whole lot of steep stairs in the first five minutes. After the stair exercise a nice woodsy stroll brings you to a gravel service road that runs up a moderately steep hill. I think that starting up the road is where the stroll ends and the hike begins, because it seems to go on and up forever. Sometimes we turn around upon reaching the road making our walk a stroll. However you hikers can continue on to the light house which is about another forty five minutes or so on gravel road the entire way. When you get to the end you are rewarded with a great view of Boundary Pass and the Canadian Gulf Islands. As a bonus the lighthouse is now a museum and if any volunteers are there you may tour for free.

    The 2-3 hr lighthouse hike is worthwhile and you should do it at least once, but it's a healthy stroll. Tip: You can access the road to the lighthouse by dinghy from the north end of Prevost Harbor and save some walking, but what kind of hike is that.

6. James Island walks stretch my definition of stroll just a little bit because by following branching trails you can spend a couple hours and climb just enough to make you very cautious in a few cliffside spots. However, you can also stroll several thirty-minute easy loops.

7. Roche Harbor Resort has expansive gardens right at the moorage and around the general area for strolling a lot or a little, whatever suits your mood.

Two places you should visit that are an easy walk. *First choice:* Follow the road alongside the big grass lawn up to the top of the property and straight across the road is the ***"Westcott Bay Nature Reserve and Sculpture Park"*** The forty or so acre park is covered with casual strolling loop trails used to exhibit sculpture art. We walk through on most visits to Roche and look forward to critiquing new exhibits with our untrained eye.

*Second choice: F*rom the sculpture garden, walk up the road past the grass airstrip and in about five minutes you will come to the ***"Afterglow Mausoleum"*** trail/service road that you have already read about in your other research of Roche Harbor. The mausoleum is back in the woods and you will see poorly maintained signs directing you along the way. If you're interested in the areas history, you will want to visit the mausoleum, and enjoy the solitude.

It's nice to go for a stroll and have a worthwhile destination. Those two places fill the need at Roche Harbor and you will be back at the boat in time for a nap. Tip, Of course you know to bring a water bottle on strolls, Right!

8. Garrison Bay is next door to Roche Harbor, and will require moving the boat, or firing up the dinghy and motoring over. It's probably too far to row with the current, but I would consider a kayak trip. With a handy visitors dock you can't go wrong adding English Camp to your strolls list, more history to absorb also.

9. Sucia: I'm not going to list Sucia as a strolling place even though we

have enjoyed many strolls because the truth is Sucia is more accurately ranked as a hiking place. Sucia Island hiking maps are available online

10. Cypress, like Sucia also ranks as a hiking place. In my opinion the biggest and best in the San Juans. I will list an easy stroll that may be converted to a bona fide hike.

Cypress Island
This easy Stroll and Bathroom stop, starts at Pelican Beach:

There is no dock at Pelican Beach so you will have to anchor or snag a buoy and then dinghy to shore. The trail to stroll starts at the conveniently located restrooms fifty feet from the beach and extend up into the woods a short way to an DNR information/interpretive site (Dept. of Natural Resources) where you will learn something worthwhile about what your seeing all around you. Next head back to the boat or continue on up the trail (now it's a hike) to Eagle Bluff (one hour up, up, up) where you will be treated to an awesome view of Rosario Strait and all the other places you have been poking around.

11. More strolls that you don't even think of but never the less need to be listed are obvious.
- A. Stroll around East Sound
- B. Stroll around La Conner
- C. Stroll around Rosario
- D. Stroll around Friday Harbor
- E. Stroll around Olga
- F. Stroll around Lopez Village (anchor

Mausoleum

and dinghy ashore, is a good breakfast or lunch plan)

Not listed as strolls are many locations that either aren't much fun or are too much work to be considered a stroll. On the next page see the hikes list for more of a workout on your cruise.

Sculpture Garden

Is hiking part of your San Juan experience?

Hiking is hard work for me and to be enjoyable requires some preparation. Going for an impromptu stroll in my flip flops and tee shirt is not a hike. Hike prep = real shoes, hat, sun-bloc, water, lunch, tri-stool, pain pills, camera, ??? most importantly a hike needs a destination worth the effort. Tip: We have hiked to Eagle Bluff many times and plan many more.

Cypress Island hiking trails

Cypress Island is number one for hiking. Some say Sucia leads for good hikes, but they are either wrong or don't consider Cypress. Maybe because it is technically in a neighboring county (Skagit County) and not a San Juan Island. Let's not dawdle, you are going to go right by or around Cypress all the time so you may as well put it on your short list.

Two enjoyable and rewarding hikes on Cypress, stand out and they both start at Pelican Beach.

First hike is Eagle bluff. The bluff overlooks Rosario Strait which means from Pelican Beach you will be hiking up and out to a promontory facing the other side of the island. Eagles ride the thermal updrafts and we have been entranced for long shows watching them soar and practice aerial attacks on each other. Once you see a bird of prey roll upside down, talons stretched to the sky, just as another raptor swoops from above in a friendly game of tag, you will become a fan like me and stay awhile at Eagle Bluff. (I've seen it referred to as Eagle Cliff on some maps)

Caution: a. You can fall off the cliff at the very top so don't let kids run too far ahead of you. b. The top half of the trail is closed until July 15th each year so nesting birds aren't disturbed.

Second hike is Smugglers Cove and is directly (almost) below Eagle Bluff. You will start out on the same trail head at Pelican Beach and part way up you will come to a fork where the *"closed until July 15ᵗʰ"* sign is located. Take the other trail towards Duck Lake through the woods and back down to the water along Rosario Strait. Along the way you will pass an overgrown falling down log cabin, of which the isolated location is a testament to a pioneering hermit like existence. The woods are as close to a rain forest as we have, except maybe the one on nearby Matia Island. The trail to Smugglers Cove will be overgrown in spots, and bringing along a pruner or lopper would be a decent public service project if you want to help out.

Both these hikes are what I would call moderate exertion and are not dangerous trails. You can walk and talk along the way assuring that any animals run and hide. If done separately each takes about 1 ½ - 2 hrs round trip if you keep moving, but you could spend an hour or so hanging out or lagging along the way. Smugglers Cove, since it's on the water, is boat accessible by running around the north tip of Cypress, but what's the point of that.

Tip: Try sitting quietly in silence and just watch for ten minutes. The wildlife is all around if you give it a chance.

Deep in the woods, on the way to Smugglers Cove

116

Hiking & Strolling

Much longer and therefore more work is the trail up to Cypress Lake. You can start at Pelican Beach if you want, but if you're already anchored at Eagle Harbor all you need do is dinghy ashore near the information station and head up the service road. Notice I said information and not pay station. That is because Cypress is DNR land and is free to camp or use the anchor buoys.

The service road trail is really a bull dozer track and goes steadily up hill at a rate that causes me to stop and rest on my tri-stool. I still rate it as moderate though because I'm the only one stopping. It's about two miles or less to Cypress Lake at about the thousand foot level and when you get there the view of trees and lake are just average, but it is a good time and place for lunch so all is not lost. On your way back down I recommend getting off the service road and taking the branching trail over to the airport and then looping back to Eagle Harbor, or taking another side trail to Cypress Head. The airport is history and has been planted with pine trees so you will not be seeing any flights out. If you peek around the trees at the end of the runway you will get a view few see. Cypress is full of connecting trails so you can access, all the lakes, the airport, or Eagle Bluff from Cypress Head, Eagle Harbor or Pelican Beach.

Tip. They keep map pamphlets posted and stocked at the information kiosks but I would not count on any being there, if you plan some extensive Cypress hiking, try to find and print a trail brochure online.

Sucia Island Hiking trails

For shear size Sucia probably beats the rest, Cypress excluded, most of the trails are very heavily trodden and some are service roads. The rangers live on the Island and drive vehicles but you probably will not see one. Sucia is flat so no real killer hills to worry about. I'm not going to outline go here or go there, just suffice it that trails connect all the bays and headlands, so you can rack up the miles if you wish. Nothing strenuous or dangerous to avoid on the trails, just wear proper shoes and have a go at them.

If you are coming by boat

DECISIONS! DECISIONS! DECISIONS!

If your arriving by boat from from the south (Seattle, Olympia) you must decide which side of Whidbey Island to travel.

The Port Townsend Admiralty Inlet side is not where I recommend you choose unless you have a good reason. One good reason would be you plan to visit Port Townsend, Port Angeles or run straight over to Victoria or Friday Harbor. Then by all means go, it is the shortest route, but it may not be the fastest. Bare in mind you may get stuck in the fog and experience rough water. You may even end up being forced to hunker down in Port Townsend while waiting for your weather window to improve. While that is not the end of the world, it may use up all your allotted vacation time.

I recommend you go up the Langley, Deception Pass side of Whidbey Island. Then when you actually get close, make the decision whether to go through Deception Pass or cut through Swinomish Channel.

The perfect solution in my opinion, is simply plan to spend the night at either the seawall berths in La Conner or Deception Pass State Park in Cornet Bay. Both destinations are about the same travel time when heading north, both offer lots of room and on shore bathrooms. If you happen to be running late, that's ok, both are open 24/7

The next day when your ready to get going you can decide whether to head through the pass or take the channel, even if you end up back tracking and going the other way (Deception Pass vs Swinomish Channel) it's only about an hour and the scenery is well worth seeing again.

Ok, ok, I feel your questions, which way is faster (shorter) and the answer is >> going through Deception Pass and right up the middle of Rosario Strait. Except we're only talking an hour or so difference, and that is mostly determined by adverse currents that are unavoidable.

What about sailing? It is unlikely you will get a favorable downwind sail to run through Swinomish Channel, so if sailing is a must your choice now becomes, head for the pass and up one of the straits.

However, you can broad reach all day long and cover many miles and still not make any progress against the current but it's sailing, right! Or with some timing on your part you can ride the current all the way to Sucia. Or Stuart.

IF YOU ARE COMING BY LAND

If your arriving by highway with a boat on a trailer, you have basically four choices that stand out. #1 Squalicum Harbor in Bellingham, #2 Cap Sante in Anacortes (sling only) #3 Cornet Bay in Deception Pass, #4 La Conner on Swinomish Channel. We have used all four (plus some others) and all have merit over others for certain situations particular to your plans. For instance, if your going to be gone a long time and want free parking, go to Squalicum, it's your only choice. Cornet Bay is a State Park and you will be left to your own devices with very little services available. La Conner is a quaint little city with a full service marina. Cap Sante has no ramp but a nice marina with RV parking where you can camp. Please read the section titled launching ramps for more details and more choices.

Tip: If you are coming for sailing by land or by sea, consider making Cornet Bay your starting point, then sail up Haro or up Rosario Straits depending on conditions and your destination, or just sail the Strait of Juan De Fuca all day and return to Cornet Bay for the night.

It is a little disappointing how many sailboats are running around with sail covers on.

119

Bring your Kayaks to Sucia Island

Almost everywhere you visit when cruising the San Juan's will be suitable for kayaks so be sure to bring them along. However, Sucia Island with all its bays, coves, nooks and crannies has miles of protected shoreline for exploring. Sucia is a veritable kayakers dream land, errr water land. Besides something for all levels and interests, It is especially well suited for beginners and young one's left to their own devices. I'm not saying to turn your hapless accident prone kids loose, but if you have normal competent children that know when to wear pfd's, then you will like Sucia. Tip give them a portable radio or walkie talkie and cut them some slack.

No Dinghy No Problem *"Just beach the boat"*

Just beach the boat! NO, NO, I'm joking, beaching your boat is probably a bad idea. But if you don't bring a dinghy to the San Juans, you will miss some of the fun.

Beaching the big boat may be easy, but you simply can't leave it there, even for just two or three minutes without risking getting stuck until the tide comes back. So consequently, you will undoubtedly skip over some cool stops and miss out. (or get stuck for six hours)

If you don't have a dinghy I strongly recommend you go buy a cheap inflatable, they are in all the department stores for $24.99 up to $89.99 for biggies. (including easy to break plastic oars, and a hand pump, and patch kit) Cheap is ok, you are only paddling a hundred feet in calm water.

Not only will a dinghy get you to shore but they entertain the kids and you may do a little exploring by dinghy too.

There are a bunch of places you will not be able to beach a boat but you could beach a dinghy or use a dinghy dock. Shallow Bay, Fossil Bay, Reid and Prevost Harbors, Roche Harbor, all would be poor choices for beaching something too big to carry.

The argument for a second dinghy

This is a valid thought and true story, and if you do a lot of boat camping with children, pay attention, this may be for you.

The evening was fast upon us as the sun made its last hurrahs at Pelican Beach and our bored son seemed extra pathetic stuck on board with his older parents so I said, why don't you take the dinghy and go ashore to one of those campfires over there. In a flash he was gone, eager to get off the boat and make new friends. Four hours later closing on midnight in total darkness we were concerned, not for his safety, not that it was dark, not that anything could possibly be amiss. We were concerned that we were trapped on the boat, totally helpless, for our son had the dinghy. How could we get to shore should we want to, how could we do anything at all if some sort of emergency arose.

In a controlled panic I furiously jammed my finger on the button, blinking my flashlight into the blackness, and then waited. A few agonizing minutes later our son appeared at the transom. "Did you want something," he said. "No, nothing," said I. "I just wondered what you were up to."

And so it became crystal clear that if multiple people are to share the dinghy when cruising, a  backup, an emergency dinghy's dinghy if you will, was needed just in case. My choice was a two man inflatable kayak for $69.95, We keep it packed and protected. I think of it as a spare dinghy that is always ready like a spare tire. It's been about five years now and the spare dinghy kayak gets used a couple times each year which justifies the purchase.

$29.95

And that's my argument for a second dinghy!

Tip: Bring a dinghy or two, or some way to get to shore.

121

All Things Dinghy

The dinghy discussion is a favorite among boaters. We certainly have experienced our share of makes and models. I won't attempt to sway your choice, like yachts there is a right time, right place and right dinghy. Then you use what you have available anyway.

Towing a dinghy in the San Juan's is the norm. The mega guy down to the open rowboat, all have reasons to be dragging along another vessel on a string. Towing your dinghy is a lot like towing a drogue or sea anchor. The definition of drogue is "vessel restraint" so towing is similar to driving your car with your foot on the brake. You can expect increased fuel consumption and a lower speed just like an adverse current or headwind.

Other thoughts on dinghy's

- Generally the faster you tow them, the more they resist.

- Multi hull dinghy's hunt back and forth forcing a super short leash be employed.

- When you stop they run into your gel coat.

- Dinghies' magically collect their own gear as if they are real boats.

- Sometimes they fill with water unexpectedly while crossing straits, or in the rain.

- Sometimes they flip over as should be expected when the wind is howling.

- Their painters will wrap around the towboats propeller.

- They get lost, stolen, jostled, overloaded, abused, disrespected, misnamed, loved, hated, sold, borrowed, rowed, sailed, raced, recycled, repaired, and become family.

We have learned more than once the hard way that problems seem to surface at the worst of times. Like the time we (not we, me) fouled our outboard prop with the dinghy towline just as we left the dock at Orcas landing. It would not have been a big deal except we drifted with a dead engine behind the ferry as it was getting ready to depart causing some concern.

Or, when we (me again) backed over our dinghy line at Jones Island while maneuvering around the float. That time coming close to bending the shaft. Then there was the time the dinghy swamped in the middle of Haro Strait from being towed too fast.

When outfitting dinghy gear for your San Juan cruise, I suggest you use a floating poly tow line for obvious referenced reasons. For me, I'm on the lookout for a lightweight floating line that will break before killing the motor or damaging the propeller and shaft the next time I mess up. For you, I offer good luck with all your dinghy adventures.

"There is nothing - absolutely nothing - half so much worth doing as

simply messing about in boats."

-The Wind in the Willows-

Properly secure your Yacht

Often we see new boaters, young and old with one or two lines holding a $50,000+ boat to the float. I can understand if they are only tying up for a few minutes, but what in the world are the others thinking? Tying the boat to the dock is simple if you follow the basics. All boats should have a minimum of four dock lines for any overnight or extended visits. Two lines act as spring lines (big X) and limit fore and aft motion at the float. Two lines (short lines) limit distance from float.

If one of the short lines fail your boat is loose so you really need to double up if you expect any problem brewing or you will be away for an extended time.

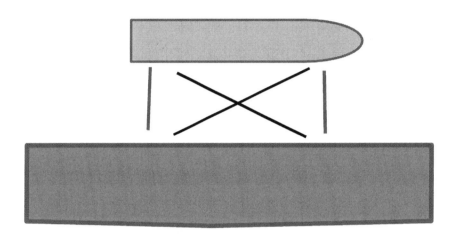

Tying to a cleat is simple and many times must be done very fast so you can get to the other end quickly. 1st take some wraps around the base, then make some criss crosses over the top. 2nd finish with twisted loops over the horns (half hitch)

Tip A well tied cleat will be fast and easy to *tie or untie* under a heavy load. Smart skippers instruct their crew how to crew.

Warning, in rough conditions, a boat slamming against its lines all night may easily chafe and part brand new 1/2" nylon line before daybreak. (Of course your awake anyway) Cushion lines with pads or hose sleeves. (or use ten extra lines)

Ten lines ?

Knowing the Ropes

Part of cruising, and boating in general includes tying your boat to the dock or anchor buoy so that it does not float away when your back is turned. Often times the skipper drives the boat into the dock (sometimes literaly) and depends on the crew to do the initial securing of the vessel. Then later he will redo or I hope check the crews work. As captain of your boat and chief cruise director you will want to make sure your crew knows what to do, how to do it, and has the necessary equipment to get it done.

Chief Cruise Director!

Dock lines need to be prepared ahead of time and be ready to go when you arrive at the float. This means one end is already tied to the correct cleat or pad eye on your boat and in the crews hand when he steps off. Notice I said step, not jump. Jumping is dangerous and not needed. The crew may hand the line to a bystander offering a hand or step off when you manuever close. NOW WHAT? They have two seconds to secure the line and grab the other end of the boat before it (your yacht) drifts away. Sound familiar? So this means a well prepared skipper has already instructed the crew how to tie to a cleat, has the lines ready, and has a boat hook ready just in case.

Once in awhile, we see a boat come in to the float that has no lines ready, no fenders, no pfd's and no clue. Then a mad scramble ensues and they are lucky someone doesn't get hurt.

There are several ways to tie to a cleat but all methods have two common characteristecs.
1. They are fast to tie and untie under a load, 2. They don't slip.

When tying to the float for the long haul, four lines are minimum. One bow, one stern line, and two spring lines.

Tip: A word to the wise again, one rough pounding night at an exposed dock will easily chafe through a brand new ½" nylon line. You need to think about chafe protection sleeves or pads, or do what I normally do which is tie a whole bunch of extra lines. Same thing for anchor buoys, discovering you are adrft in the dark in thin water is no way to get a good nights sleep.

Overheard at the dock:
"I don't know "*#*#," it was right there when I left."

And some other things not related to holidays.

Throughout the San Juan area are navigation aids to help prudent skippers safely arrive at their chosen destination. Probably the most used and useful aids are buoys marking safe passages. The age old mariner saying or nautical mnemonic is the **3 R's, "Red, Right, Returning"** and if you don't already know this you have been under a rock, but let's not point any fingers at the mate or crew.

Red Right Returning (3 R's) means, keep the red aids on the right when returning from sea. So if you're traveling away from the ocean, up river, into a port or some other place, like entering a cove, then you're returning from the sea. Down river, departing a place or out to sea is not returning. Got it, only two directions, so you need to know which way you're headed in order to know if that buoy should be passed on the right or left. There are many places where you will see pairs of red and green markers indicating a channel, and your safe course is in the middle, and the red is on the right if you're coming home. Way out in the wide open places will be a solitary red or green or black or striped marker at the end of an island or headland and you will not have any idea what it means. For our purposes, they mean heads up and pay attention. This is when you need to locate on your chart or gps your exact location and determine a safe course. They didn't put the aid out there for the fun of it.

Tip: Some aids will be marking shallow water and you must not cut corners thinking your boat only draws two feet and you can sneak through. If you insist on short cuts then slow down to a speed that will not cause damage when you hit, and there is no speed that doesn't damage a spinning propeller. We have found that our gps and charts allow us to gunk hole in really thin rock strewn bays, but we have paid the price and taken our share of punches. A warning word about gps charts is needed. Some aren't accurate in all spots, a giveaway is when they show your boat traveling on dry land when you are sure you're in the water. Don't fall into the trap where you think your gps chart is right on the money in one area so it must be ok in all other areas. It's simply not the case, your gps charts have mistakes and you need to be suspicious and vigilant when nearing potential disaster situations.

Tip: Going dead slow or listening to the mate and turning around is a prudent course of action. (but, I would never suggest not gunk holing)

When traveling from one park to another, you need to get away from shore, your chart and your depth sounder are your primary navigation aids and help you stay in deep water, a beginner's mistake is to safely travel fifteen miles and then run aground at your destination because you were too close to shore. It is tempting to run close to shore like a gawking tourist enthralled with the sights and then thud the party's over. So either run dead slow or move out into deeper water. I feel uncomfortable and get tingly when the depth is less than thirty feet and we are in unknown waters. When the bottom gets up to about fifteen feet from my investment, I slow down and start paying close attention demanding my crew be quiet and help keep close watch ahead. I know whispering is probably pointless and Capt. Bligh like, but every time we/I get in a jackpot we are noisily doing something distracting from good boating practice, so I try to keep focused while we circle islands and gawk at the scenery.

Just for the fun of it, add this other nautical mnemonic to your data base.
"A good red wine is port" *(not true) but it will remind you that a boats red and green running lights are arranged with the red light on the port side! Got it! Now when you see that vessel at night out in the distance you will know which way it is pointed, and remember the 3 r's* ***"Red, Right, Returning"***

What is red and green with rocks all around?
Pretend this is color and then drive your boat between the buoys.

This is the entrance to Shallow Bay, you darn well better not short cut here.
China Caves are in the background cliffs (in the trees)

The system in use doles out camping space whether it be on land, at the float, or in the water, is a variation of the old finders keepers rule, or as some like to say first come first served.

What this means to me and you is that all camp sites, all anchor buoys, all wide open anchorage space, and room at the float is up for grabs. It may get a little dicey at times. Sometimes when a boat leaves and a space opens up there is a scramble amongst anchored boats, each skipper wanting the vacated space. Sometimes someone has been stationed on the float to claim ownership of the empty space, or they may have asked another boater to wave off perspective tenants while they hoist anchor and move over to the float.

In keeping with the first come idea, you are not supposed to hold or reserve an anchor buoy by tying your dinghy to it, but we see it done all the time while a boat is out fishing or running for provisions. As a practical matter, using an anchor buoy is not much of a benefit, if any at all, over using your own anchor. In fact after seeing anchor buoys fail and float away at two locations I am very cautious and back down on buoys just like setting my anchor as a way of testing their integrity.

When you arrive at your destination, go right to the dock and claim any space that's empty. Tip Its ok to let your boat hang out past the end of the float, so that end spot that looks too small may hold you after all. If you don't want float space, you may lay claim to any unoccupied anchor buoys. The official marking for anchor buoys is a blue stripe, but some are a looking a little tired, or they had no blue paint that day. All the parks have kiosks on shore for making payment.

You may anchor for free (yes free) anywhere you want. In fact, it's ok to anchor anywhere in the state unless there are signs prohibiting anchoring. There are a few small marked areas where eel grass is protected and anchoring is frowned upon and quite possibly illegal. (mostly at Echo Bay and Eastsound) When anchoring pay attention to your swing and make sure you don't encroach on someone already in place. Remember the finders keepers rule, it applies to anchoring just the same. If someone lays claim to a perfect setting and is already anchored, you must stay clear of their 360 degree circle. And if bad things happen and someone must move a boat, it will be the last one in that's the first one out. That's the generally accepted rule the world over. Tip See section on "Anchoring tips."

More Docking/Anchoring Etiquette

Note: We see all the time, skippers that are not prepared to come into the dock so I will list off some points to ponder.

1. The float is where accidents are likely; consider having your crew put on a pfd. while docking.

2. Have your fenders out before your final approach.

Docking/Anchoring Etiquette

3.   Have your dock lines attached and ready to hand to someone on the float. You would be surprised how many boaters are not ready with lines when other boaters are extending a helping hand.

4.   Long jumping is not advised. If your crew is unable to easily step off, you should come around and try again.

5.   Do you have a boat hook? It should be out and ready for action. If you don't have a boat hook you should get one or carry a stick with a ??? for snagging things.

6.   It is a very good habit to pause dead in the water safely clear of the dock so you can judge how the wind and current affect your boat, this way you may abort or change your approach before trouble surprises you.

7.   Put on a smile, go slow, you are about to meet your new neighbors.

8.   And if you ever watch your wake, this is the time to be extra careful not to rock someone.

Tip: See section, "Knowing the Ropes," for tips on tying your yacht
so it won't get away or damaged.

Once you arrive it is common for other skippers to comment on how well you handled docking, which makes you swell with pride. On the other hand, a bungled maneuver may be met with silence, which just makes you wonder. My favorite comment to hear is, "It looks like you have done that before." Once at Langley, on a particularly difficult day, someone came up to me when I was standing on the dock and said to me, "Your son did a good job."

Holding Tanks

There is nowhere except across the line in Canada where you are allowed to dump your holding tank and I'm not sure the Canadians still allow it so you should plan on holding it. All the marinas and resorts maintain pump out facilities, but none of the parks have any pump out systems. All the parks have composting toilets, but you may need to plan on visiting marinas for potty breaks and pump outs if you have picky people on board that don't like privies.

No Dumping

We have one on the boat, but this is much bigger!

VHS Marine Radio

I am wishy washy on the need for a radio. On one hand, if an emergency arises, it is the accepted means of communication out on the water, but chances are you will not use yours, or at least not need to use it. However, the radio is a good source of entertainment, it seems a lot of cruisers can't be quiet and must constantly keep in touch discussing eta's, which side to hang fenders, when to start the chicken, and of course the all important sun-downers.

If you don't have a radio already, and don't really see one on your ski/camper/fishing/party boat in the future, I suggest you pick up a $99 portable handheld. There are several available and some bounce and float, which probably will seem like a good idea after you have dropped it over the side. Think of it as insurance, and you can always call the Harbor Master for a slip assignment.

If your cruising with children and anticipate they will be hiking or exploring by themselves in the dinghy, you should again consider a portable just for them. Then they can call you when they get stuck nearby or want you to bring them lunch. A set of quality walkie talkies will suffice with the children, your choice.

You should know that your cell phone will work well in most areas, and probably will be your first choice when problems sneak up on you, but no promises.

Sunrise Somewhere

Off shore Anchoring for runabouts and shallow draft sailboats.

We see a lot of boats on the beach, (intentionally)mostly dinghy's and kayaks, but a fair amount of bigger boats too. Some will bring their boat to James Island, or Jones or Cypress and run them ashore planning for the outgoing tide to strand them until they are ready to float off in a day or two or three or four on a rising tide. If leaving your schedule to mother nature works and your boat is suitable, go for it, but if you plan to depart on your schedule you will want to keep the bottom of the boat in deep water most of the time.

No Dinghy No Problem, just beach the boat, unload your gear,
then move it out into deep water, and swim to shore.
Here's a simple way to beat the falling/rising tide.

First, I strongly recommend you acquire a dinghy, you don't have to carry it on your boat, you can tow it the entire time. Car top it to the San Juans and back home.

The solution

If you insist on traveling down the highway without a spare tire you may have an equally good reason for cruising without a dinghy and you can always anchor out with an anchor system designed to let you pull your boat back into deep water after unloading your camping gear.

You will need an anchor that you set in deep water farther out than you plan to park the boat. (don't forget you need some scope)(see anchoring gear section) You will need a turning block attached to a float or fender, and enough line to run to shore above high water and back to the boat. That's it.

Disclaimer: I'm not doing this for you, just giving you an idea, you are doing it for yourself. I'm a firm believer that if someone needs help figuring out how to accomplish rigging, jury rigging, mickey mouse, untested, unknown, or a myriad of other little life's challenges, then perhaps they shouldn't be attempting anything I suggest. If I just rattled your cage, don't sweat it, you probably are much smarter than others and know when to seek competent help.

Most of you will recognize this system as nothing more than a marinized version of the old continuous clothesline loop on a pulley.

In the proverbial nutshell, this is how to do it.

First set your anchor further out than you plan your boat to be sitting. Rig the anchor with proper scope and a float or fender attached to a turning block or pulley (carabineer) of some sort. (The bigger the better because it will probably get gummed with seaweed) You need enough line to run from the pulley to shore and back just like the clothesline on pulleys.. On shore you will need to find or create another strong point (an anchor, sand screw or log will do) Stretch the loop between the two anchor points Now you can pull the boat back and forth by rotating the loop. Don't forget to take into account high tide, making sure your land attachment point is out of the water.

132

You need to know that the scenario just outlined is fraught with potential problems. (you will have extra line to deal with) Other boaters may run over your line. (The pulley will get jammed) We all know that the more we complicate things the more we screw up, so here's a few pointers, but I bet the screw ups still happen. The only reason I'm going along with this is that I know this is how some of your best boating vacation story's are created, and it is unlikely anyone will get hurt, just lose their dignity.

Here are some minor little points learned by doing, or lessons learned the hard way. First off don't let your line get stuck or jammed in the turning block. Remember your boat will wander back and forth all night. Don't let your outboard, drive, keel, rudder, etc. get hung up on your turning pulley fender float. You can remedy this wandering by tying fore and aft or using a bridle, but that opens you up to catching wind or current, which means make darn sure the anchor is set well. (you must always, always, expect wind to come up at anytime, period) I have seen really long strong bungees used and they work well, but that seems costly. A turning block made from a biner might open on you (make sure it locks) and they cause a little friction. Don't use a rope that kinks easy like twisted stranded poly or pretty much any three strand. Braided poly kept taught at all times is what I've seen work good. Don't pull the boat out further than necessary, you may have to go wading or swimming. Sometimes your crew will not hold on to the bitter end when pulling the boat back out (oops). Another problem that comes up is that your 500 foot anchor rode doesn't lend itself very well to this job. We have two low tides and two high tides, make sure you plan for the correct tide, most of the time our really low tides are in the daytime, so at night there is less of an issue than in the day. One last thought, many runabouts and swing keelers can be left on the beach without concern, but you will be stuck until rising tide and people will constantly ask you if ran aground on purpose. So that's it, if you really are set on beaching your boat overnight, that's one way to make it work. What could possibly go wrong?

Some people new to cruising may never have anchored their boats even though they have years or decades of experience. If your new to boating you may benefit from a few ideas shot across your bow.

"How well you sleep is proportional to how well you anchor"

One anchor is simply not enough. You should bring a minimum of two anchors. Some old salts have four or more. NO no don't use four anchors at the same time. I mean bring them with you. Anchors and ground tackle are not like a spare tire or emergency brake in your car. For cruising, anchors and assorted gear are more like dock lines and fenders that you use all the time. Gear needs to be in good shape, stowed ready to deploy, and you need to have a passing familiarity with their usage so that you can properly instruct your crew. When parking your yacht for the day or night you will undoubtedly be really, really close to shore in shallow water. That means when things go south, they will go south in a hurry and expensive damage or even scary dangerous situations can crop up and ruin your cruise in a heartbeat.

Now that I have focused your attention let's talk shop. This guide is for boat camping in the San Juan's, not setting up your boat for hurricanes and world travel. Remember we assume you are a prudent and competent skipper in all things related to your boat. Your main anchor rode should have five or more feet of chain, simply tying a rope to your shiny new anchor is cutting a chafed corner a bit too close. That chunk of chain is important for all sorts of reasons and we will leave it at that. You will be anchoring in ten to twenty feet of water so you need five to seven times that in rode length. Therefore, one hundred feet of anchor line is ok, but two hundred feet would be much better.

"When anchoring, bigger is better"

"**Reality check,**" You will you be anchoring in Roche Harbor and It's forty feet deep or more in places where you might want to spend some time. That hundred foot line is going to be inadequate when the wind tops twenty five mph and your at a 2.5 to 1 scope. If you cut your anchor line for some reason, (let's see, it's wrapped around the prop, its stuck under a rock, you need some dock line, you need to tie to shore, a tow line, someone ran over it and its wrapped around their prop) you will be glad you have some extra line.

Tip Not only should you have lots of line, but it is a very good idea to have your second anchor, anchor chain and rode already assembled and ready to use in an emergency situation. We keep our extra set ups in bags so that they stay tangle free, and easy to grab out of storage.

A second anchor, when deployed will help you keep the boat from swinging in a crowd, and if you use your dinghy to carry a second anchor out into deeper water, you can pull your boat further out when you discover the tide is dropping more than you expected. Generally, having second or third anchors available will make you feel more secure in all things related to keeping your

investment floating and away from the rocks. In addition, when you lose your primary anchor (snagged on a rock) your secondary will be pressed into service. For that reason alone, your second anchor should be as robust as your first. Some people will have a tiny little lunch hook that doubles as a dinghy anchor; we have one too and rarely dig it out, but we still have it.

Our anchor rode is visibly marked with red spray can paint at the fifty foot, hundred foot, and the one fifty point. When I anchor I look for fifteen to twenty feet depth, and then lower (don't toss) the anchor while the boat drifts backward. When my anchor touches bottom I try to pay out the rode slowly at first so that the chain lays on the sea floor in a line instead of a pile on top of the anchor. (We have thirty five feet of chain) I then let the boats momentum (or put her in reverse) pull out rode to the one hundred foot mark. This next part is the most important. I cleat the line hard and fast so that the boats momentum yanks it taut setting the hook. (setting means, dig the flukes in) If I don't feel that snap jerking the boat to a halt, I use the motor to put some pressure on it. If I still don't get a taut line, I start over.   When starting over for another attempt it means moving the boat back into position in front of all the other cruisers intently watching, so this is your chance to show your stuff, or how you handle frustration.

Tip, you should pull the anchor up to the surface and clean the mud and grass off the flukes or it may never set properly.

 Depending on the situation I will many times set a second anchor 180 degrees away from the first to catch the reverse tidal current or wind shift. To do this I will let out another hundred or more feet of rode letting the boat drift back to where I lower the second hook. Then I painstakingly use my electric windless (very painful)(you could motor but be careful of fouling the prop) to set the second anchor while pulling the boat back to where I want it. (in the middle) When using two anchors it is sometimes desirable to tie one fore and one aft to hold the boat straight in position, but be very careful when doing this stunt because the boat will act like a sail catching wind and current instead of swinging free. The added force may break or jamb gear, or even pull out your anchors.   Anytime the wind or current gangs up on your tackle you are going to lose the fight, so your boat must be allowed to swing free when the going gets rough. *In plain English, when using two anchors you should run both anchor lines to the bow if you are in doubt.* Some books will tell you that you need 7 to 1, or 5 to 1 scope, some say 3 to 1 if good conditions.   I always initially set the anchor at a long scope and then reel her in to a much shorter scope after I am positive my anchor is dug in well. You must decide what the proper scope is depending on all conditions. If your boat breaks loose in the middle of the night it is an emergency, your the skipper, and that's, that, period.

.

"Why is it called the bitter end?"

More points to ponder

Loud, obnoxious, boisterous, yelling or cursing are no way to announce ones arrival to an anchorage. I am on my good behavior, since I will never get another chance to make that first impression.

Defensive Boating

Defensive boating, is just like in your car, you need to be prepared to move when a boat comes at you dragging its anchor. Watch others upstream/upwind of you when they anchor, if they don't have much scope out, or didn't set their anchor, watch out. Tip Its better to move your boat in the daylight before they drag into you in the dark.

Anchor lights:

If your in an established anchorage, (all parks are) you don't need to have a light, but if you think someone may run into you, turn it on, that's the smart call. To save electricity I sometimes use a battery powered light run up a halyard, plus if we are on shore after dark, it makes finding the boat easier. More than once we have shoved off in the dinghy heading back the boat and not been able to see it in the dark. On *Kraken* our newest San Juan boat we use solar powered yard lights.

Muddy Anchor Syndrome

Bang bang, bang bang. My god, what's that banging? It sounds like something is beating a hole in the boat.

Is it just me or do others hang their anchors in the water to let the boats motion wash them clean?

It's 7 am or earlier, and I weigh anchor for no good reason and get under way. Hot coffee in one hand, tiller in the other, a glorious sunrise, I have better things to do than swish swash my anchor a hundred times trying to get the darn thing clean of mud. So I hang it suspended just below the surface and motor off dead slow, just coffee and me. Second cup, third cup, I speed up, bang bang, bang bang, the anchor is reminding me that's its clean and ready to be stowed, or I should I say, slow down before it destroys any more gel coat.

And that's how all those little dings got there, courtesy of the

-Muddy Anchor Syndrome-.

"Better to be poor on sea than rich on land"

Not all places are listed

This guide is for boaters cruising the San Juans and surrounding area. Unfortunately, many of the areas sights and attractions are not accessible or just don't promote themselves in the marine direction. If an Island, park, or resort is not listed, it is because we didn't think it was suitable for inclusion. That doesn't mean that the place is no good or that you need not pay it a visit. It simply means that we felt it was not somewhere you would care about while boating about.

This anchor buoy sign at Cypress Island says it cannot
be reserved with a dinghy

Mileage Chart

Rosario…………..ROS
Roche Hbr….   ..RH
Sucia……….. …. .SUC
La Conner………..LAC
Squalicum Hbr….SQU
Stuart Is…………STU
Saddlebag ………SDL
Deer Harbor…….DRH
Blind Bay… …….BLB

Cap Sante…………..CAP
Pelican Beach………..PB
Blakely's…………….BLK
James Is……….…....JMS
Jones Is……….…..JOS
Fisherman Bay………FSB
Cornet Bay…………..COR
Friday Hbr………..…..FRY

	ROS	JOS	RH	SUC	LAC	SQU	STU	SDL	DRH	BLB	CAP	PB	BLK	JMS	FSB	COR	FRY
ROS		11	16	18	25.5	21	17.5	16	10	6	17	8	4	9	8.5	19	10.5
JOS	11		5	10	29.5	27.5	6.5	22	2.5	5	21.5	14.5	9.5	13.5	8.5	23.5	6
RH	16	5		14.5	34	32	4	27	7.5	10	26	19	14.5	18	12.5	29	10
SUC	18	10	14.5		27	19	12.5	16.5	12	15	21	12.5	15	17	21	21	16.5
LAC	25.5	29.5	34	27		23	36	9	28	24	9.5	16	19.5	16.5	26.5	9	27.5
SQU	21	27.5	32	19	23		31	14	25	22	16	13	17.5	19	24	25	26.5
STU	17.5	6.5	4	12.5	36	31		28.5	9	11	21	21	16	19	14	29	11.5
SDL	16	22	27	16.5	9	14	28.5		20.5	17	2.5	7.5	12.5	9.5	18.5	17.5	21
DRH	10	2.5	7.5	12	28	25	9	20.5		4	19	13	8	11.5	8	21	5.5
BLB	6	5	10	15	24	22	11	15.5	4		16	9	4.5	8	5	18	7
CAP	17	21.5	26	21	9.5	16	21	2.5	19	16		8.5	11	8.5	17	13	19.5
PB	8	14	19	14.5	16	13	21	7.5	13	9	8.5		4.5	8	11	15	13.5
BLK	4	9.5	14.5	15	19.5	17.5	16	12.5	8	5	11	4.5		5.5	6.5	15	8.5
JMS	9	13.5	18	17	16.5	19	19	9.5	11.5	8	8.5	8	5.5		9.5	9.5	12
FSB	8.5	8.5	12.5	21	26.5	24	14	18.5	8	5	17	11	6.5	9.5		19.5	4
COR	19	23.5	29	21	9	25	29	17.5	21	18	13	15	15	9.5	19.5		22
FRY	10.5	6	10	16.5	27.5	26.5	11.5	21	5	7	19.5	13.5	8.5	12	4	22	

Made in the USA
Lexington, KY
01 July 2017